The Courage to Shine

Find Your Voice and
Discover the Healing Power of Your Words

For April

Keeping it fun on the edge!

By
Dr Eileen Forrestal MB Bch BAO FFARCSI

Eileen

The Courage to Shine

First Printed in United Kingdom 2021

Published by Conscious Dreams Publishing
www.consciousdreamspublishing.com

Edited by Lee Dickinson and Daniella Blechner

Typeset by Oksana Kosovan

ISBN: 978-1-913674-47-2

Dedication

Dedicated to Bridie, my mum

Acknowledgements

I thank my mother for being my mother and the source of my life.

I thank Jewel Carter who asked me that question.

I thank Patricia Fitzsimons for inviting me to listen to something new.

I thank Werner Erhard for his powerful seminars.

I thank Jeff Wilmore for seeing me hiding.

I thank Douglas for walking with me, step by step, up the mountain.

I thank Emily G for believing I had a story worth telling.

I thank Gerard Beirne for bringing order to my thinking.

I thank Roger James Hamilton for igniting my entrepreneurial 'genius'.

I thank Jack Canfield for the encouragement to shine my light.

I thank Dr Mark Mathews for his wise soundings.

I thank Daniella Blechner at Conscious Dreams Publishing for her patience as we brought my private conscious dream into public view.

I thank everyone, and you are too numerous to mention, for the part you played in my story. You know who you are. Without you, it would have been a very different story.

Contents

Foreword

Eileen Forrestal brings a new meaning to the word COURAGE – the courage to ask yourself the tough questions: Who am I? What am I here for? And the courage to act on the answers.

I first met Eileen at one on my workshops when she was looking for advice on how best to introduce her *Get Up and Go Diaries* into the United States.

I fell in love with her very original and special diaries because they are so full of great inspirational quotes and messages.

And now, in this book, she has stepped up, bravely walked through her fears and is sharing her own personal story. And what a powerful story it is.

You see Eileen wasn't always as brave as she is today. Today she is a bright, bubbly, smiling woman, confident and happy, spreading her inspirational message of forgive the past, live fully in the present and create the future you want for yourself and others. Knowing the Eileen I know today, it's hard for me to imagine that she had suffered in silence for so many years, paralysed by her fear of SPEAKING.

This wonderfully written book brings us full circle on her journey beginning as a bright, bubbly, excited child, to her experience as an unexpectedly traumatised child, to a quiet, withdrawn teenager and young adult, through lonely and frustrated middle years, and then back to the bright, bubbly excited woman she is today. And the best part, is that on that journey she accumulated a wealth of wisdom that she shares with us, based around the theme of how to break through one's fears, and limiting beliefs by cultivating the courage to speak up and speak out, and in so doing, she inspires all of us to do the same.

This book started as a silent promise she made to her mother to not 'die with her music still inside her.' This wasn't a promise that was easy to keep, but it's one that gave her the determination to courageously struggle, and finally to succeed, to find the hero inside herself.

One of Eileen's favourite quotes is by Joseph Campbell: 'The cave you fear to enter holds the treasure you seek.' Eileen chose to enter a cave she feared and she found that treasure, and now she offers the secret of her discovery to you, her readers. In the process she 'saved' herself and this book shows you how you can also save yourself.

As a Medical Doctor, Eileen was all too familiar with treating the diseases that resulted from the damaging coping behaviours that snuffed out the light of too many, too early in life. She has seen too many people go down the path of resignation and despair – from suppression, and repression to depression. Unfortunately, she has seen too many people die with their music still inside them.

This precious book that you now hold in your hands will help you to discover the music within you and encourage you to express it in your own unique way, to ensure a happier, more enjoyable and more fulfilling life.

Fortunately for you, Eileen Forrestal, who (as an Anaesthesiologist) spent 20 years putting people to sleep is now in the business of waking others up. And when you finish reading this book, you will be one of those people – awake, aware and ready to add your voice to the chorus of those people who have chosen to live and experience life to the fullest.

– Jack Canfield
Co-author of the *Chicken Soup for the Soul* series and *The Success Principles: How to Get from Where You Are to Where You Want to Be.*

Introduction

I started to write this book when I realised my mother was dying. As her only daughter, with no children of my own, I was reflecting on who I was and what was I doing with my 'one wild and precious life.' (Mary Oliver) What had I done so far with the life she had gifted me with? What would be an acknowledgment of her contribution? What could I do in the future, in the absence of motherhood, that would allow me to shine as she did, and fulfil her desire for me to be happy in the world? What would me being happy look like?

I was in a swimming pool, having just taught my friend Jewel to swim, helping her to overcome a fear of drowning that she'd had since childhood, when I was confronted with the question, "What are *you* afraid of?"

'Nothing,' I answered, honestly, as I had already overcome my fear of 'speaking'.

"Everyone is afraid of something," she persisted.

As she looked straight into my eyes, compelling the truth, tears of awareness welled up from somewhere within my soul and I heard my self say: "I'm afraid of dying without ever having been known".

"Oh, that's easy," she said cheerfully. "Write a book."

I was in Bali, on a month's leave from my job as a Consultant Anaesthetist in a Regional General Hospital in the Northwest of Ireland. I was exploring a new opportunity in the world of entrepreneurship and speculating on a future of global impact through expansion of the small publishing company that I had co-founded around five years earlier.

My mother, who knew me better than anyone in the world, was 88, with failing health. She had just moved into a nursing home, after living with me for eighteen months, and was facing an entirely different, and predictable, future. Her job was done. I considered maybe mine was only starting. I promised my friend that I would write my book.

This is it.

It's a story about a girl's journey to discover the words her voice wanted to say but couldn't (or wouldn't) say. It's a story of a girl who suppressed her voice, withheld those important words from the person she loved most in the world, why she did this and the impact it had on her life.

It tells the story of the accidental events that happened up to a pivotal point in my life, the purposeful events that followed, and the underlying thread that marked the inner journey of turning points, which could only be connected by joining the dots backwards. It traces the events and decisions from my childhood, through adolescence and into early adulthood, that shaped my life and my relationships. These laid the foundation for my successes and failures, all in an effort to hide my fundamental failure – the failure to express myself – the result of a speech impediment, my stammer.

This is the story of my struggle to find my voice – and then the courage to use it. What did I really want to say? It was as if some smaller voice inside me was calling ... like something unsaid that was demanding to be expressed, and I had to say it, and in the saying of it, and calling me to something bigger, something else disappeared.

What disappeared was the silence, the silence in which I had suffered, and the suffering that was trapped in the story. The telling of the story was sufficient to liberate me from its grip, freeing me up to write a new story, with a new perspective, for a new life, with a new future, inspired by my own words, with no suffering required! This then, is the whole story; the truth, the whole truth, and nothing but the truth – my truth!

This is a journey from the heart to the head and back to the heart, and finding the courage to identify and overcome the fear that stopped me, the fear of being known, of being seen and heard for who I really am, the fear of hearing myself speak, and having nothing to say; the fear of being nobody that anybody wanted, the fear of loving and not being loved and losing it all.

I got trapped in a life I wound up in, a life I had designed for myself. 'The cave you fear to enter holds the treasure you seek'. Yes, it took courage to go back and investigate my story, to acknowledge my crime, to confess my guilt, to seek forgiveness, and to say the things I never said. It takes courage to be the adult in your own life, to take the reins from the upset child, to master the art of living graciously, to get in the driving seat and set your own course to a future you want, to live a life of your own design.

If I wanted a different life, I would first have to have the courage to let go of who I had become, unwittingly, and then to create my life from choice. As George Bernard Shaw is quoted as saying, 'Life isn't about finding yourself; it's about creating yourself.'

I chose freedom and self-expression. This book is a result of those choices.

And then the doubt?

What if I got it wrong? What if I messed up? What if I failed? What if there was no one else to blame? "Most people don't want freedom. Freedom requires responsibility and most people are frightened of responsibility" (Sigmund Freud). I was no different.

Such was the start of the adventure. And in the saying of that, and the living of that, I get to shine.

This is the purpose of this book – that you find the courage to set yourself free from whatever dulls your sparkle, from whatever has stopped you from living your 'one wild and precious life', shining in the art of living.

So, who am I writing this book for? For you the reader, in the hope that it will encourage you to follow your own dreams, to not die with your music still inside you, to explore any hidden areas of your untold story, where your life stopped singing, and start shining. And for myself. They say the most important book you read in your life is the one you write yourself! So, yes, the writing of this book was a gift to myself, in giving me permission to 'tell one on myself', freeing me from all the drama I had added to my life. For my mother. Yes. In love and gratitude. I now accept myself as she accepted me. In those last few years, I had finally become the person she "hoped I would be when I when I was three". She got what she wanted; a happy daughter.

The book has two parts: the first part, the bulk of the book, tells the story of my early years, growing up with a speech impediment, 'abnormal' in a normal family. My journey of 'hide – and – seek', of escaping and seeking self-expression in other ways, provided the backdrop for an extraordinary life, constituted by a colourful career, incredible adventures on my many travels, and the wisdom gleaned from all those experiences. The second part comprises some important things I wanted to say ... that took me a long time to say.

Woven into the narrative is the underlying relationship I had with my mother and how that impacted all my other relationships, including, fundamentally, the one I had with myself.

It took a certain degree of courage to identify, and overcome, the fear that stopped me in life: the fear of being known, of being seen and heard as whom I really am, the fear of hearing myself speak, and having nothing important to say. That fear kept me hidden and silent for a long time. I explore this concept of courage from a personal perspective, but maybe it provides a universal view.

You will also discover how the power of words – in speaking and in listening – the said and the unsaid – can create and destroy, can punish and forgive, can hurt and can heal. This is a story of failure, revenge, encouragement, forgiveness, liberation, empowerment and the triumph of love over fear.

For many years it felt safe and 'comfortable', to hide in the shadows, like a cocoon from which I would someday emerge – butterfly-like – and fly free. I waited. That day was not coming. It became tight in the bud. How could I get out where I could live and breathe, free to be me? I didn't want to die a caterpillar. What if I could become the butterfly?

Self-expression is essential to life. There are many like me who live like we have no voice, suffering in a particular kind of silence, in the silence of the unsaid, believing what we say doesn't matter, that our word has no power.

It's not true I had no voice. I had a voice; I simply didn't use it.

I simply lacked the courage to use it.

I did speak.

I said "I can't and don't ask me" … and under my breath, by way of warning, in the unsaid but clearly communicated … "and if you do, you'll be sorry!".

I said "I have nothing to say".

I said "It doesn't matter."

I said "I don't care."

I said "Go away and leave me alone, I don't need you. I hate you".

I lied.

I didn't say "Stop it, you're scaring me."

I didn't say "What's wrong with me?'

I didn't say "I'm sorry, it's all my fault".

I didn't say "I'm scared, I love you. Do you still love me??"

That would have been the truth. That could have set me free.

But the lie was the life I lived. And that lie was the torch that lit the way for me, it led me here, to this page. Without that lie, without the 'suffering' I endured, without the struggle and effort I put into surviving that lie, my life wouldn't be the one between the pages of this book. I'd be living some other life, somewhere else. And I wouldn't be sharing this story with you.

The written word was always easy for me. Writing my story came easy for me. I simply told the truth. It has not been easy, but it has been utterly rewarding. It is no accident that the heart is the seat of courage, for when we let go of the fear and let in the love, life becomes a complete joy. When we look at the world through loving and trusting eyes, it is a different place.

My particular journey is unique to me, but the destination is the same for all of us. The more of it we can travel with our eyes open, the more we will enjoy the journey. My journey was not as conventional as it could have been. Without the lie I was so desperate to escape from, it might have been a lot less interesting, or maybe more interesting, who knows. This was the only life I had. I created the drama, and suffered it, for what? To prove what I knew? "I can't. It doesn't matter. I don't care"? I suffered in the drama of the stuff I made up, and like a really good actor, I got stuck in the role in a gripping movie – that gripped me. Maybe you don't have to suffer either. Maybe suffering really is a choice.

My choices never occurred as choices at the time; they occurred as the only option. I had to take each step and choose it later. Knowing it took every step to get here, if I had to live my life over, I would not change a thing. It took everything to get me here, every last tiny element of my life. If any one thing had changed, everything could have changed. I am grateful for all of it, the good the bad and the ugly; it means I have something valuable to say, that it's all perfect the way it is, always.

I now get to live a life free of all that drama, free to make new choices. I escaped from the role I'd outgrown, a role that no longer defined me, reading from a script that no longer expressed who I was, to exit the movie I was trapped in. Like a prisoner being released after a prolonged life sentence, into a whole new world, I was free to create a new role for myself, in a new movie, as an author in my own life.

How did I get out?

I stopped and looked and listened.

I listened to the script.

I didn't like what I heard.

I wanted a different script, and that was the truth.

That was the only way out of the lie.

There were many truths and lies to discover. The digging had to be done. And I needed to do the digging, all the way down, into those dark places I didn't want to go, to uncover what was buried deep down there.

Was I ready? Was I willing? Was I able?

I knew something had to change.

If not now, then when?

I risked it.

I felt the fear and did it anyway.

I explored the fears that were driving my life: the fear of being misunderstood, of not being listened to, not being heard, not being important, or wanted, or loved, and saw them as fears. Nothing more.

When I told the truth about all that, suddenly there was an opportunity to be free of it, and I took it.

I wrote the book in silent promise to my beautiful mother that "I will not die with my 'music' still inside me".

This is my opportunity to have my music, my voice, heard out here in the world. Maybe you, in reading this book, will be encouraged, or inspired, or empowered to say something, or do something, in your life, that will have you shine in the world.

The exploration of my own life's journey has been one of endless discoveries, challenges and rewards. Exploring the universe within is no small thing. I was discovering I was a mystery even to myself. I was exploring my own humanity, not just the life and times of Eileen Forrestal. If I wanted to solve the mystery of who I was, and how I came to be the person I ended up being, maybe I could also solve the mystery of who others were for me, of who we all were for each other, and how we got that way? Was it all simply by accident?

This is a book for anyone who feels like there is something missing in your life. It's for those of you who, like me, have allowed some fear to keep you from showing up, from speaking up, from shining as your true self. Sometimes we know the fear that stops us in our tracks – be it spiders or flying or strangers; sometimes we don't. We are all subject to fear. We don't often stop to ask where this fear comes from. Why this fear? Why not that fear? We know the fear limits us in some way, but we navigate our lives around it. We manage. We avoid spiders and flying and strangers. However, we may be unaware that we're stopped from being fully ourselves. We just live within its confines – a small, safe and comfortable life.

Maybe we tell ourselves we're not afraid of anything, we simply ''can't' or 'don't want to' do it. "I can't deal with strangers." "I don't want to fly anywhere." "Dogs are dangerous" Therein might lie the lie … and we're afraid to admit it. We love our justifications and we will always find our evidence!

As human beings, most of our fears are universal. They relate to the fear of loss: loss of love, of belonging, respect, status, possessions, health, youth and beauty. We also fear being judged and criticised. We fear failing. We fear being rejected or ostracised. We also fear the unknown. No matter where you go in the world, one or more of these fears will not be too far beneath the surface of everyone you meet. Some fears are clearly visible on people's faces or in the way they hold their bodies or the way they react. Some are well disguised.

The only thing we all need in the face of fear is courage. Courage to face the fear. When we don't identify fear, or admit to it, we don't need courage. We pretend we're not afraid, we pretend we're comfortable and life is perfect, and we've got it all handled, we're in control, prepared. We live small, safe, careful lives. We follow the script. We know how the movie goes. And then BANG, life happens! A relationship ends, illness strikes, the business fails, war breaks out. "This wasn't in the script!" Now what?

This is a book about courage. The courage to find out who you really are, what you really want, and what you're truly capable of. The road to happiness is an inward journey. It requires the courage to go inwards, to explore the depths of yourself, to go back and retrace the steps, the turning points, on your own journey to where you are now. We can only go forward from here, and we need a vision of the future to guide us. Looking for a road map from the past will not help. Discovering how we got here might enlighten us as to how and where we went off track. We know we can't go back and create a new beginning, but we can start here and design a new ending. We can let ourselves be pulled by what we love, rather than driven by what we fear. Our dreams can be the blueprints of life's coming attractions!

There are important questions to be addressed.

How many of our dreams have we given up on?

How many of our tomorrows are spoiled by something from yesterday?

How many goals or dreams are put off for one more day?

How much of our lives simply pass us by while we wait for something better to come along? How much do we not notice? How much do we take for granted? How often do we say, "not now" and wait for better weather, a better opportunity, a better time or a better reason? Time spent waiting for the script to change, for the 'trailer' to end and the real movie to start, the one you really want to star in. Tomorrow. Waiting. For a time when we're more confident, more courageous, more willing, more able, then ... then we'll do what we've always wanted to do.

Life passes by quickly. As we get older, the fear that life is passing us by, becomes very real. This is the tomorrow we dreamed about yesterday. Time waits for no man or woman. Carpe diem.

I discovered that I didn't have to live today with the ghosts of yesterday. I could put the ghosts of yesterday to rest in peace. I realised all my ghosts were fears from the past.

When we can face our fears with courage, we can see them for the truth of what they are – fears, ghosts or shadows – we then have an opportunity to embrace them as fuel for courage and move on. They won't go away entirely but they can lose their grip. We also need to have compassion for our lack of courage. We must learn to forgive ourselves. It's okay to let the past be. It need have no further hold on us. We can be free to live in the here and now, fully present, unencumbered, open and curious. Now we can see and hear what is going on around us. Now we can have some real power. Now we can choose freely. Now we can act in accordance with how we want life to go for the future. There's nothing to fear in the future. It hasn't happened yet. We can have a say in how it goes. We can be the author, the scriptwriter and the director, and we will still only be but one of the many actors in our movie. We get to play the role we choose for ourselves. We get to say our lines and leave space for the next character to enter the stage, as we dance to the music we set in the background of our life's unfolding movie.

Words matter.

What we say matters.

This book explores the power of language and the domination of silence.

This quote sums up how silence occurred for me; not as the quiet reflective silence of choice but the silence of withholding, of domination, of not saying what wanted to be said. I was complicit in my own silence.

"Silence, they say, is the voice of complicity. But silence is impossible. Silence screams. Silence is a message, just as doing nothing is an act.

Let who you are ring out and resonate in every word and every deed. There is no sidestepping your own being or your own responsibility.

What you do is who you are.

You are your own comeuppance.

You become your own message

You are the message." ~ **Leonard Peletier**

We're each responsible for our own self-expression.

This is mine.

Thank you for being here. You're in the perfect place.

You've landed into the middle of my life.

You'll discover much about me as we go through the following pages. I discovered a lot about myself as I wrote these words. My intention is that, in reading them, you're empowered, entertained, enlightened, encouraged, inspired. That's what writing them did for me.

So, if I feel that what I say is important and I want to be heard, what happens if you're not listening. What if my words fall on deaf ears? What if you read this and go away with nothing new, and I have not contributed anything to your life, what is it all for?

Without your listening, my words are silent. So I ask you to be my perfect reader. I want you to be curious. I want you to be willing to look at your own life – perhaps ask yourself is there something missing, like a piece of the jigsaw, and if you want that missing piece. You might want freedom or clarity, or ease, or peace of mind, and to know how you can get it. All I know is how I got it, so if it's possible for me, consider it's possible for you too. It may even be somewhere in this book. Keep reading until you find what you need and read more to find what you want.

There are no magic wands or miracles here, simply words. That's the power of words. I want the time you spend reading this book to be worth it for you. I encourage you to have the courage to travel the inward journey that I have taken. I want you to be willing to discover something newly about yourself. You can of course simply skip through the pages, jumping to the interesting bits and ignoring other parts; but perhaps in these unfamiliar parts, there are words or sentences that could have real value for you, and open up something you don't already know, those parts that sit outside your comfort zone, those areas where, if explored, much of your own fulfilment and peace of mind will be found.

For now, I ask you to get present to the realities of your own life, like I had to get present to the realities of mine, my lived, day to day, life, and ask yourself some tough questions: – Where are you? How did you get here? Is this where you want to be? And where are you heading? Are you on track? Are you driving the train, or are you a passenger? What's the destination? Is the train stopped? Who's on the train with you and do you all want to go to the same place? Are you still standing at the station, waiting for the train? Do you need to get off the train? What could happen if you tried to get off this one? What train could you get on? Is the light at the end of the tunnel an oncoming train? Is there something you need to say?

The quality of our lives depends a lot on the quality of conversations we have with the people in our lives, and the relationships we have with these people. We are one of these people. We talk to ourselves a lot. And we listen to what we say. Sometimes we need to look at the questions we ask ourselves – and listen to how we answer them.

Here I am, having asked and answered some tough questions, happily living my life and happy to tell the tale. I am very grateful for the 'lie' I lived, that gave me such an interesting and successful life, and some hugely valuable lessons. As I looked back, I could appreciate those great moments, but as lived, it lacked something. My experience was that somehow it was small, smaller than the life I was capable of living. So, while I did everything to try and enlarge it ... the missing piece of the jigsaw eluded me. I found it where I wasn't looking. I didn't find it in more and more adventures or travels or new countries or new experiences, I found it where I least expected, where it was all along. Was I simply afraid to look, fearing there might be nothing there? I found it in my heart when I finally found the courage to look there. And I found it as it came out of my mouth. I am now living life from the inside out, and loving it. For the most part, it's my same old life, but I'm a new me, at one with myself, where the outside of me finally matches the inside. It might have been a painful labour to birth me, but I now love who I am, and that's the truth. The journey was worth it. I am now free to live life on my terms. I feel the lowly caterpillar is now flying as light as a butterfly.

I'm living a big life. Where I go from here is up to me. Where you go is up to you. We all have a say in our own future.

After a 32 year career in medicine, where I spent 20 years 'putting people to sleep', I am now enjoying my entrepreneurial endeavours where I am now more interested in 'waking people up'. I have transitioned from 'healing hands' in medicine to 'healing words' in publishing – with the unfailing desire to heal hearts and minds, and alleviate the suffering in the world. "Sticks and stones will break my bones...," but punishing words can hurt for a long time!! What if we used our words with care?

With a new found freedom of self-expression, and the courage to shine, I have an exciting new arena in which to play, and a new game to win. There is a new world I want us to build – a world that works for everyone – where we use the true power of our words to build each other up, one encouraging word at a time.

Until I found my own voice, and the courage to use it, my experience of my life was that it was small and insignificant, despite all my accomplishments. That is not the truth. This is simply how I occurred for myself. It is not who I am. I am a work in progress.

We are each a work in progress. My invitation is that you stop hiding the gift that you are and express it and share it with those you love. Have the courage to shine your own light.

Another favourite quote of mine, "Don't ask what the world needs. Ask yourself what makes you come alive and go do that. What the world needs is people who have come alive." ~ **Howard Thurman**

Let this book ignite your inner flame. Let who you are shine brightly, lighting up your life. Because the world needs you lit up. Alone we can do so little, together we can light up the world.

CHAPTER 1

What Happened?

"I'm not upset that you lied to me. I'm upset that from now on I can't believe you" – **Friedrich Nietzsche**

Someone once remarked how strange it was that I ended up in a career as an anaesthetist that involved putting tubes down people's throats! Perhaps it was no accident, given that my first interaction with the medical world – hospitals, doctors, nurses – was to have a tube stuck down my own throat and my stomach pumped after an accidental overdose of aspirin, aged three-and-a-half.

My 'story' goes that, while playing hide and seek (my favourite game), on finding a great hiding place between the high shelves of the pantry, I discovered a "bottle of sweeties", and excitedly offered to share my treasure with my older brother (by fourteen months). Being that bit wiser, he wasn't too sure it was such a good idea, so without hesitation, I took them all for myself, and swallowed them whole – in case he changed his mind!

Within a very short time my crime was discovered by my brother or more likely by the tell-tale evidence on my yellow-stained, lips and tongue. Immediately, I was whisked off to Temple Street Children's Hospital, Dublin, where I was handed over by my distraught mother to a "black doctor and a nun", neither of whom I'd ever seen before, who proceeded to empty my stomach of the forty or so junior aspirin.

I can only assume I was probably terrified at the unfolding drama but, having no memory of this event, I relied solely on my mother's recollection. She'd been a children's nurse before she married, so was acutely aware of the gravity of my accidental overdose, and also likely equally terrified. She knew the danger I was in. I didn't. My distress was at being inexplicably separated from my mother, not knowing what I'd done, while hers was at the thought of being permanently separated from me if I died.

Fortunately, I survived the ordeal with no immediate ill effects. However, this heralded the start of what was to become the central drama of my young life – my stammer.

It started obviously enough with retching and vomiting, then coughing and choking – it wasn't my fault, I didn't mean it, I wasn't a bad girl. Through sobbing and tears, a jumbled mess of gibberish poured out of my mouth – I tried to explain.

I tried to apologise. She seemed so upset. "I didn't mean it. I'm sorry." She seemed inconsolable. Was what I'd done so terrible? She didn't seem to be listening. She didn't want to hear what I was trying to say. I would have to show her. I needed her to know I wasn't a bad girl. I'd show her I could be very good, and I'd never cause such trouble again.

It was a simple plan, an obvious solution to make up for all the trouble I caused. It would surely avoid such pain in the future; my own, and the awful, bewildering distress of my beloved mother.

She remained upset. I knew it was all my fault. I was sorry, really sorry; I didn't mean to cause all that distress. Why was she still crying? I was there? They didn't kill me, I didn't die. Why was she so upset? At that age, my whole world revolved around me. Everything became about me and my attempts to console, to speak and explain about what had happened. I failed miserably. The words got caught and I choked and retched and spluttered and cried. And so began a lifelong battle to make myself understood.

This 'incident of the tablets' became part of our family folklore and was accepted as the justifiable cause of the infamous stammer that was to plague my life. I was left in no doubt as to whose fault it was – my mother's confessed guilt told me everything! She blamed herself for her carelessness and was racked with guilt for many years. It was too easy for me to blame her.

Perhaps I blamed myself too. With hindsight, and insight, it's possible that, in my three-year-old world, I believed I was being punished fairly for a terrible mistake. I obviously wasn't aware of my 'wrongdoing' nor its consequences at the time of ingestion, but in the moment they were trying to help me vomit them up, my full attention was focused on my survival. It's likely I believed they were trying to kill me, and I was trying desperately to save myself – as it seemed like there was no one else there to save me! Did I even have an anaesthetic? Was I fighting the mask and resisting being rendered unconscious by these strangers in this strange and hostile place? Did I simply have a tube forced down my throat, without anaesthesia, to remove the tablets?

I have no answers to these questions. No matter. Whatever they did, for sure I was traumatised in some way. We all were.

At that age, obviously, I had no awareness of death but, no doubt, self-preservation exists on many levels. Survival is paramount, and I survived. However, I think the terror that my young self was unable to express, became an anger I directed at my mother – "how could you let them do that to me – hurt me?" Hurt, fear, betrayal, vulnerability, weakness, shame, guilt – the seeds were sown.

So what was the impact? Was this single event, of which I've no memory, a pivotal determinant of the course of my life and a significant influence on my relationship with myself, my family and the world? It certainly coloured my relationship with my mother for many years. She didn't listen. I couldn't trust her to be there for me in times of crisis.

Could I trust myself to recognise danger, or to not do something so careless in the future? Could I trust the world? It was a dangerous place.

My father? Where was he when I needed him?

Doctors and nurses were frightening, but they did take care of me. I didn't die. If I had to rely on someone, perhaps these were a better bet than my family!

What I didn't understand, until many years later, was the connection between my 'accident' and my mother, at thirty-seven years old, actually suffering the loss of another baby around the same time. I vaguely knew there was a new baby coming, but my brother never made it home from hospital – he lived a week, then died. So while my mother was grieving the loss of her baby, I was still in the world of believing it was all my fault and I could make her happy by 'being good'.

But it wasn't working. She was inconsolable. I wasn't enough. She wanted this (dead) baby boy, that nobody had ever met, not the (live) baby girl she already had, who was strong and brave, had survived the hospital and was here, helping and being good. I needed to be more helpful and better at being good, so she'd forget that baby boy who wasn't here.

Anyway, my plan worked for a while. I was a good, nice, well-behaved and helpful little girl: an "angelic" child, a credit to my parents, who could take me anywhere.

Apart from this constant choking and coughing and retching and words getting caught in my mouth, life was good.

Then there was talk of tonsils.

Despite outward appearances, I remained quite upset after my traumatic ordeal, and the speech difficulties with stammering and stuttering and anxiety continued to cause concern at school.

By the time I was six-and-a-half, it was decided that removing my tonsils would help. I couldn't see that there was any connection between my words and these "tonsils". "What are tonsils, anyway?" I had a vague idea of where they were, as the doctor had looked into the back of my throat with a torch and a wooden stick many times, making me retch. However, I knew my tonsils had nothing to do with me not getting my words out. The sounds were clearly stuck in the middle of my mouth, on my tongue somewhere, so I thought no more about that.

However, the stage was set for another life-changing moment! My mother told me I was going 'on my "holidays"'. She obviously wanted to spare me the anxiety of another traumatic hospital ordeal, so I was blissfully unaware of any plot that was hatching.

I knew about holidays. I loved holidays. I was such a good girl now, the best! This was my reward. I happily headed off, the memory of my previous ordeal obviously more prominent in her mind than in mine. There would be no mention of the word "hospital".

I was going on "holiday", to a "hotel"! I packed my small suitcase with toys and books and headed off excitedly. The (private) hospital looked very much like what I expected a hotel to be. I arrive in my 'hotel room' and pick my bed. It seems a bit strange that there's a girl from my class in school on another bed, in my hotel room, on my holiday, but that was OK too. What did I know about hotels?

When she said she was having her tonsils out, I happily replied: "Well, I'm not. I'm on my holidays," and proceeded to play with my books and dolls.

Needless to say, the following day – when strange things are happening all around me and I'm wheeled on a hard narrow bed down a long corridor to a room with bright lights, and I wake up with an agonising and merciless, searing pain in my throat – I know things aren't going well.

I'm frightened, upset and in bewildering pain. I lash out at everyone. I'm furious and it's too sore to scream, but I scream anyway. I'm forced into silence by the agony in my throat. How could she?! SHE lied to me! She did it again! She let them hurt me. The betrayal was overwhelming. And, to add insult to injury, my classmate had known all along. I felt embarrassed and stupid – and in excruciating pain!

My aunt arrived with a gift to appease me – a beautiful black baby doll with a colourful 'grass' skirt and multi-coloured beads on her wrists and ankles – I wasn't going to be bought off by that – I took the doll and tore it apart and flung it to the four corners of the room.

I'd figure this out myself. She lied. I wanted revenge. I'd 'get her'!

Ice cream, jelly – they all went the same way. I wouldn't be consoled by 'trifles'. My world had been shattered, and they thought ice cream would make it better. They were all in it together. Again. They hurt me, and SHE let them! SHE lied. SHE was NOT to be trusted.

In an instant, I came to certain realisations – adults lie, especially those who tell you they "love" you! And you can't trust people – especially those who say they love you. That's just a trick so they can hurt you. I'd show them! I didn't need them. I didn't want them. I didn't want HER. I didn't need her.

She tried to console me. I was having none of it. My revenge was swift and immediate:

"Go away. I hate you!"

An upset, six-year-old child, with no view other than her own, had made a shattering 'discovery' – a realisation. They were 'bad', and I was 'good'. It was like black and white. I was right and she was wrong. She shouldn't have done that! I would have to figure this out for myself.

"I don't want you and I don't need you. I hate you." In that moment, alone and afraid, I could trust no one. I felt utterly betrayed.

In that one instance, I took my love and trust away from my mother, the source of my life, and I broke her heart. I didn't discover until years later that, in that same moment of distress, I'd also broken my own.

As for my father: where was he when I needed him? Again, he'd failed to protect me. I'd show him I could look after myself. I didn't need any of them. I was nearly seven.

As for my classmate, how did she know? I should've known. I would have to make sure in the future I knew exactly what was happening, so I'd be never caught not knowing as publicly as that again. Question everything. This was a better decision. I would learn a lot about the world with my endless questioning of everything. I had a kind and well-informed father, albeit 'weak', and an entire education system and library at my disposal. I wouldn't be caught wanting again! I'd listen and learn, and I'd know everything!

Of course, the interpretations of an upset, six-year-old child may be very valid, and understandable, at the time. Unfortunately, I believed my conclusions about myself (I was stupid), about people (especially my mother – she didn't love me), and about the world (it was a hurtful place), were the truth. This all settled somewhere in the back of my subconscious but was to have many ramifications for me throughout my life, impacting all of my relationships.

Anyway, after the incident of 'the tonsils', whatever stammer I had before that became noticeably worse. I didn't want to speak anywhere, to anyone, and especially not to HER. I was too hurt and upset and angry. It was all just too difficult and shameful. My guilt was there for all to 'hear' when I opened my mouth. That 'bad girl' who swallowed the tablets – this was my punishment!

So, while I subconsciously wanted to punish her for the suffering she caused me, she was also punishing herself with guilt for her failure to prevent the overdose – and suffering in the world of being 'a bad mother' – and I took advantage.

The more she tried to get me to calm down and speak properly, the more I stammered, the more frustrated she got and the more upset I got. I struggled at school. I struggled at home. All the children in the neighbourhood were now happily stammering along with me, but they could stop, and I couldn't. My misery grew. There were more speech therapists and child psychologists, to no avail. Was my unconscious desire to be right about my mother and punish her for what she did more powerful than any desire to speak properly?

Or did my fear of speaking properly hide a deeper fear of growing up – alone, unloved and unwanted – and actually being afraid of what would come out of my mouth? If I were to tell the truth, what would that be? Would I have to admit that I'd lied, that maybe I was wrong and I didn't blame her? Could I forgive her, tell her I loved her, and that I was sorry for the trouble I caused and for punishing her by taking my love away, and that I missed her?

Perhaps. But that's not how I saw it. She was wrong and I was right about that. We both were.

The drama continued, my anxiety escalated, the stammer worsened. I turned to my silent world of books and my pets for comfort. I retreated from the light as best I could, making myself small and unobtrusive, hoping no one would notice me. I did my homework diligently; I was quietly defiant but no trouble to the teachers. I was attentive. I listened closely to what they were teaching. If I could just stay silent, hide and pretend I was normal, like all the other girls. With my best friend at my side, I had my 'partner in crime'– she knew when to intervene to save me from being exposed as the fraud I was.

At sixteen, when I mentioned to the career guidance teacher I was considering medicine, there was general agreement it was utterly unsuitable as I "would be unable to talk to patients".

My general determination and rebelliousness however, won out. I convinced my family of my firm belief that, if I could 'hide' in college for seven years (and medicine was the longest course) without the stress of telephones, I'd be able to overcome this stupid stammer, and become a 'normal person'.

On some level, yes, this is what happened. I figured out a way to work the system so I could still manage to get away with what I got away with for so long. I discovered there was no real need to speak up, and I avoided any occasion to do so. This meant I could look normal.

I already knew that nobody can make anybody do anything – if they are willing to take the consequences. I was. In fact, it gave me some personal satisfaction to see how well I could manipulate the system to get what I wanted. Or what I thought I wanted.

CHAPTER 2

Trapped

"The only real prison is fear, and the only real freedom is freedom from fear" – ***Aung San Suu Kyi***

True to my plan, I went straight into medical school at seventeen, to University College Dublin. I had lots of acceptable reasons for doing medicine. I had enough points in my Leaving Certificate.[1] It was certain to be interesting and I knew it was well within my capabilities. It sounded good when I said it to other people. My two best friends were going, and, most importantly, it was the longest course in college. My teenage defiance occurred as a triumph! In my young world, it would simply provide the necessary temporary relief; a 'teenage strategy' to deal with the shame of embarrassment.

How would that work in the adult world? I'd cross that bridge when I came to it.

---

1   The Leaving Certificate commonly referred to as the Leaving Cert is the final exam of the Irish secondary school system and the university entrance examination in Ireland

For me, what mattered was the thought of being able to sit in a classroom and be taught for seven years and not have anxiety around speaking.

This is actually what I believed. My older brother had gone to college a year earlier and he said lectures were great: you just sat there, listened, took notes and left. Exams were at the end of the year. No one asked you questions. No one expected you to speak. Wow! That was the most delicious music to my ears. I could do this with my eyes (and mouth) closed!

I loved learning, I loved school, I just hated that I was different and shy and quiet and all the things that I wasn't inside, and didn't want to be, ever. But I was stuck inside this person. School was a place where the teacher asked questions and you had to give the right answer. I didn't ever care if the answer was right or wrong if I could simply answer – anything. But I couldn't. Not like everyone else could, that is. Not with words that made sense even if they were the incorrect answer. I suffered in a prison from which there was no escape, my words trapped. I was trapped. How could I get out? How could I escape the prison of silence or, worse, the horror of lies if they were easier to say. Of course, I knew the answer, but it was easier to say "IIIIII dddddddddddddddddddddddddddonntt know" and sit down, much to everyone's relief and embarrassment, most acutely my own. Or say "America" because I couldn't say Germany, or take out a sweet or chewing gum and be sent to the head nun's office for being disobedient, and feel even more of a coward and a traitor to myself. Imagine seven years where I didn't have to endure that torment: the anxiety, the daily reminder of my inadequacy, the fear of being expected, or pressurised, to speak.

I thought I'd found a clever solution when I was around thirteen.

I arrived in school one day to find a substitute mathematics teacher replacing my regular teacher. I was slowly 'training' my regular teachers to ignore me – I was doing OK. In fact, I was doing surprisingly well. I'd no problem with learning, understanding, reading and writing. I was hungry to learn new things. I loved listening to how the teachers spoke so knowledgeably and easily explained things. Left alone to learn, the occasions for speech and mutual embarrassment, were minimal.

But this guy was new. I was apprehensive. I had back-up – my best friend, who sat beside me, was always ready to jump in and answer any question and save me. Would she be able to save me today?

He started to move around the room, asking everyone their name in turn. He started at the back. I always sat at the front. He had a system. He went along the rows, one, by one, by one. I could hear everyone say their name and sit down. I knew my turn was coming. The anxiety was mounting. What if my friend couldn't save me here? I was sitting in the front, my usual place, my heart pounding, my palms sweating, my mouth dry, my tongue starting to stick to the roof of my mouth. I could feel my face starting to burn red with the inevitability of it all. Please stop. Please let the bell ring. Please let the fire alarm go off. I prayed frantically – please let me faint. Or die. Please someone come and stop him.

And it was suddenly my turn. He is there, towering over me. I can smell the cigarette on his breath. His teeth are stained. His face has an ugly grimace as he sneers at my obvious distress, enjoying his moment of power.

He asked the question. I couldn't even hear it. I was deafened by the pounding of my heart in my ears. He asked it again – my friend answered.

"I didn't ask you," he spat and, turning directly to me and pointing his finger in my face: "I asked HER."

He glared at me, demanding an answer. I wanted to run for the door, but I was frozen: my legs like iron bars, feet glued to the floor. I was trapped. He asked the question again.

"What is your name?"

I start ... but my mouth is too dry. My tongue is too big and stuck. My throat is closed. The tears that started at the back of my eyes start to roll down my cheeks. The anger, resentment, hatred, helplessness, the hopelessness, the injustice of it all. But what hope did I have?

"MMMM IIIIIIIIIIIIIIIIIII NNNNNN CCCCCCCCC CCCC CCCCCCCCDDDD DDDDDDDDCCCCC CCCC DDDD..."

It all ended in horrifying bewilderment for both of us. The class was silent. And then I heard it: the coughs, sniggering, suppressed laughter. Was it mocking? Embarrassment? Pity? shame? Who knows? Who cares?

That was it. I'd had it. I finally accepted defeat. I couldn't do this anymore. Then I made a powerful decision: 'No. I would simply refuse. I won't do it. He can't make me speak. Nobody can.'

And I got it. My power. Silence!

"Answer me!"

No.

I refused. I realised this was now a battle of wills. Silence. I relaxed. A peace came over me – and I knew I'd won! Would he beat it out of me? He could try – I wouldn't give in. He didn't try. My resistance had won: the silence of domination, and he was powerless against me. My silence screamed at him: 'I WILL NOT SPEAK TO YOU.'

He knew he'd lost this one. He moved on. I sat down, triumphant. There and then, in an instant, I invented a new mantra for myself. It was a realisation, a statement, a powerful sentence: "They can shoot me, they can jail me, but they cannot make me speak." I'd show them all. I will NOT speak in class again.

And I promised myself I'd never have to speak anywhere again. I wouldn't speak if I didn't want to. I wouldn't bother trying to 'speak properly' any more. I was done. I'd show them who was the powerful one. They could do their worst.

And so, out of my 13-year-old thoughts came the design of my life! A life sentence! One that no one but me heard. And thus, was laid another foundation stone for the evolving story of my life.

The pressure was off. I'd won. I'd never have to speak in public again. The relief. The triumph. The answer to all my prayers, and I'd invented it. Silence. The perfect solution. For now! I might pay the price later, but that would be later. I was too elated by my own ingenuity and drunk on my own power to realise what I'd done.

I didn't realise I'd just sold my soul to the devil. I'd given up. I'd sold out on my voice. I'd sold out on myself in a moment of blind panic. I'd sold out on my own self-expression. I sentenced myself to a prison of my own making and threw away the key. I would now live my life sentence, a 'half-life', and surrender to the cost.

At thirteen, I disappeared. At thirteen, the Eileen Forrestal I was ceased to exist. Another Eileen Forrestal appeared: a sullen, sulky, silent teenager, who hated herself even more. Other people spoke for me. I waited for others to speak and hopefully say what I might have wanted to say. I still had the freckled face that went bright red at the thought of something that might cause me to be embarrassed, which was everything, and now, along with no voice, I had braces, few friends, a flat chest, no boyfriend, and a feeling of hopelessness that I'd ever be normal. If depression had been an option in those days, I'm sure I would've had it. But it wasn't, so I got really good at pretending all was well and that I didn't care. I lied, and people believed me.

I sold out on myself at thirteen. My words became meaningless. I became a consummate liar. I just wanted to speak words to sound normal – I didn't care if I spoke the truth or not. The truth didn't matter. What mattered was that I sounded like everyone else. So I copied them. I said what they said, the way they said it. I watched as words fell from their mouths. I faded into the shadows. I didn't trust myself with my words as I'd no words of my own. Without our words, what have we? Who are we? How do we impact the world? I didn't know who I was, and I'd no say in the matter.

Self-expression is essential to life. Without it we live in a particular kind of silence, the silence of suppression, of repression, the noisy silence of the unsaid. Just because the words don't get out doesn't mean they're not screaming to be heard, out there in the world: I'm here, I exist, I matter, I have something to say, please listen to me.

And so my inner life began to separate from my outer life, and it seemed like never the twain would meet. The outer lie and the inner truth – or was it the other way around? This was now the beginning of my half-lived life, or my life lived in two halves, seemingly one disconnected from the other; who I was for myself, and who I was for others. And yet I looked and sounded completely normal, just like everyone else!

Little did I realise, in my triumph, I had simply traded one trap for another.

I was always trapped in the same thing. I was trapped in this Eileen Forrestal, and I hated her. I hated that she couldn't speak properly, that she was sullen and shy; that she couldn't join in with normal fun; that she couldn't dream of having a boyfriend or ever being normal in the world. So I fought with 'HER'. I lashed out at 'HER'. I simply directed all my anger at my mother. It was all 'HER' fault, after all.

*****

I vividly remember the day I first realised I was trapped.

I was around eight years old. I had a new coat. It was fawn with brown buttons and a belt around the waist. I thought it was lovely, soft, stylish. I was walking down the road to the shops. I was wondering if my friend, also called Eileen, would like my coat, even envy it. Maybe I'd meet her on the way.

And I suddenly stopped, struck by a sick realisation in the pit of my stomach. I would never be that other Eileen. I would always be this Eileen. Eileen Forrestal: this horrible, stupid, angry, stuttering, Eileen Forrestal; "the girl with the stammer", 'the stutterer'. The word made no difference. Whatever you chose to call it, for me it was a betrayal, and it killed off my life. *It* didn't say what I wanted or needed it to say. *It* didn't say it the way it should, or could be said, the way other people said it, so effortlessly, fluently, easily, normally. *It* was different. *It* always got the attention. *It* got the reaction, not what I said. *It* caused the embarrassment. *It* got pity. *It* made people sorry for me and want to help – or to turn away. I knew I was different. I wasn't stupid. I just got excited, and my words got stuck. "Oh, the poor child," as they waited, patiently or impatiently, or rushed to help me get my words out. "Slow down. Breathe. Relax."

But it was pointless. The words were stuck. Stuck in my throat like a hammer, with unintelligible sounds emanating from me like a machine gun. And I coughed, and choked, and retched and, cried.

Without my voice, who was I? Trapped. Betrayed by my own voice. Suffering in silence – and tricked into lying.

I stood there, on the path, holding back the tears. What did it matter? Who cared who I was anyway? It was hopeless. I'd carry on, smile, be nice, and maybe no one would know how lonely, nasty, horrible and unlovable I really was. I don't remember if I ever made it to the shops.

*****

At seventeen, I was determined to prove my decision and my plan to be right.

48

I discovered early on that there was no real need to speak in public, and I avoided any occasion to do so. Plenty of others were very keen to have their voices heard, and I was happy to encourage them. While I could control the occasions, once there, I couldn't control the fear, and it was the fear that started to control me. The fear said what I could and couldn't say and do. If I was confronted, my initial reaction was to escape. If I couldn't escape, mostly I lied. I made up stories of how I wouldn't be available, or I convinced someone else to step into my place. Or, worse again, I said I'd do it, and simply didn't turn up, hoping to be forgiven later.

Every lie was justified in my own mind. It was a matter of survival. Life in medical school became very much a game of resistance, avoidance and pretence. The fear kept me 'safe', or so I thought. Safe from embarrassment. Safe from humiliation. Safe from being seen and heard as the 'fraud' I was.

I cleverly managed to get away with what I got away with, every time. But, in order to get away with it, to hide what I was so desperate to hide, I had to come up with more and more elaborate excuses. The fear kept me small, hidden, silent, unknown and alone.

Nobody can make anybody do anything they don't want to. We can't even make ourselves do what we don't want to. And we suffer the consequences regardless. We punish ourselves and then we suffer. We suffer and then we punish ourselves. We think we have free will. What we mostly express is our free 'won't'. And it seemed like I was willing to take the consequences of what I wouldn't do. I was caught in a game of trying to 'triumph' in a vicious punishment-suffering cycle, quite unaware of the hold it had on my life. I'll punish you for asking me to do something I can't do, and I'll suffer in my justifications of why I can't do it. I'll punish myself for not being able to do it and I'll make you suffer by not giving you what you want. I'll suffer in my silence and I'll punish you by withholding myself from you.

I was becoming someone I didn't recognise. I was slowly becoming someone else, now hidden even from myself. I wasn't a happy person. I was winning the game I was playing, but it was just a crazy game thought up by an upset thirteen-year-old and set to play out across multiple ages and stages of my life.

As usual, I did well in my exams and, on completion of my Finals, I got a place in my teaching hospital, the Mater Misericordiae. During my first six months' internship, the unthinkable happened: I lost my job.

No one thought you could lose your job as a doctor, but this was the early eighties, and the country was in the grip of a severe economic recession. My brother had already emigrated to Canada.

I'd taken a holiday in November, to visit him, when there was an announcement of redundancies in the Mater Hospital. They were cutting four posts. It never occurred to me I'd be one of the four. I did nothing. A friend advised me to come back and 'fight' for my job. I didn't see the necessity of that. MY job wasn't in danger, surely...?

It was! I was cut.

When I asked afterwards why my job had been cut, given my high academic record, the response was, "you didn't fight for it!"

As luck would have it, the following February, after failing to find any vacancy in Ireland, I found myself in Hove, Sussex, England, in a tiny district general hospital affiliated with the Royal Sussex County Hospital in Brighton. This was a turning point in my life. I hadn't been best pleased at having to go to England but, if I hadn't been forced to leave Ireland at that time, the world may never have opened up for me like it did. I was forced to learn how to survive, on my own, in a strange country.

When I left Ireland and entered the real world of work in England, life became more complicated. There were more occasions where my speaking was expected. I was by now, however, practised and skilled at hiding. When hiding wasn't an option, plan B kicked in and I left. I moved from job to job, hospital to hospital. Fortunately, medicine is like that. Moving around every six months was considered normal, so it wasn't noticed. I just had to survive for six months before I was noticed. I worked hard, was meticulous, conscientious, nice and obliging. I was bright and had no difficulty passing my exams. I learnt everything. My knowledge and skills were superb. But, for me, over the years, it was exhausting, proving my worth and hiding my true self, fearing to speak and wondering how long it would take before I was really found out and sent home.

But I was never found out. I became more and more successful. I didn't get any happier. I'd become a prisoner of my own character, a victim of my own success, in my own drama, and it never occurred to me to play a different character in a different play I could just as easily have thought up!

The fact is all I could see was the satisfaction I got by manipulating the system to get me what I thought I wanted. I just didn't know what I wanted. All I really wanted was freedom, the freedom to be who I was, and that was never going to happen. Each 'escape' occurred as a personal triumph, but subconsciously I was suffering deeply, knowing that somewhere I was selling out on myself. I knew my life was smaller than it could or should've been. I knew I was trapped in a vicious circle, but knowing I was trapped didn't help – I didn't know how to get out. I was trapped in the prison of my own thinking, and there seemed no way out of that one (or so I thought!). How could I escape from myself, trapped by my own voice, betrayed into silence, not opening my mouth so the betraying liar couldn't get out? That was the prison: the silence, the refusal to speak, the trapdoor shut, with me inside, always waiting for someone with a key to open the door and let me out.

Working in England, I soon discovered that even though we all spoke English, we most certainly didn't speak the same language. All the nuances and connotations and understandings were lost. I was lost, for a long time. I worked hard. I made mistakes. Not medical mistakes, just mistakes in reading people, communication mistakes. I tried to make friends. I found myself with the other 'foreigners'; as there were very few Irish people. I met the Indian and Pakistani doctors, the Iraqi, Australian, South African, even Burmese. I learnt about these distant countries and tasted their wonderful food. They were friendly and polite and generous, and we shared the camaraderie of being foreign. I made good friends.

It wasn't a good time to be Irish in Britain. In October 1984, when I was in working in Brighton A+E, I'd just gone on leave. I'd no sooner left the airport when the Brighton bomb exploded.

After two weeks of the anonymity and freedom of travelling in some Far East country, my true escape, I returned to hostility. I was locked into my Irish identity, betrayed by my voice, my accent: a criminal by association, a victim of history, this time trapped in the listening, but trapped all the same.

They say the way out of the trap is to accept the trap. I accepted the trap. I could escape any time I wanted by leaving the country. Slowly, I made my own way, deciding how I wanted to be viewed as an Irish person in England, much as I did on all my travels. The Brighton bombing was pivotal to my growing awareness of identity. I was a peacemaker at heart, and always wanted to share all the good that Irish people have been known for, the world over, for centuries. I was now ashamed. And yet part of me understood the desperation for independence, for self-determination, the human desire for freedom from oppression, and the extent people will go to, to punish those they believe are the cause of their suffering. There had to be a better way.

I listened to all the anger. I knew it wasn't personal to me. I heard what they said. Of course, I understood. My dad had always said to us, growing up, that when we looked at other people and thought we were so different, "there but for the grace of God, go I." I could've been born into any one of their shoes. I'd then have their life and their view of the world. I'd then quite likely think the way they thought and do what they were doing. We were all just reacting to our circumstances and trapped in our reactions.

Over the years, I've worked in many different countries and in different areas of medicine, but the training of those early days in the NHS was invaluable and stood me in good stead. The confidence and independence I gained were priceless. While part of my identity was trapped in the past, each time I moved, it was an opportunity to reinvent myself. No one knew me. It was a big world. I could hide, and I could explore, and I could lose myself, in order to find myself. I still didn't speak much, but I listened a lot. I was curious as to what other people did. I compensated for not speaking by trying out these new things. Sometimes they were crazy, even dangerous things, but always exciting and pushing me to test my limits. Horse riding and rollercoaster rides became my favourite activities!

I slowly freed myself up from the constraints of my past – my family and friends at home who 'knew me', by the way I had trained them to know me! I had to learn to adapt. I had to 'grow up'. I had to discover who I was out of the shadow of my past. Each time I returned home, it seemed like I was more and more a different person to when I left. Of course, I was. None of us remain unchanged after an experience. However, with all my running, I was also growing further away from something else: myself!

I worked in many different areas of medicine in those early years. I trained as a general practitioner, with anaesthesia and obstetrics, with the specific intention of going to work in Africa, and with the option to carry on as a GP on my return. I didn't get an opportunity to use my training in the developing world to the extent I would've liked, as the prevalence of AIDS limited my options, and when I did return from Zambia, after eight months in Lusaka, I settled back into Ireland and anaesthesia.

Looking back at all the 'turning points' in my life, they all had the element of escape. But, as they say, there's no escape; out of the frying pan into the fire. I'm sure I tried to escape from my captors who were holding me down to anaesthetise me to pump my stomach after I swallowed those pills as a child. Perhaps I thought I could escape having my tonsils out by simply ignoring or denying the reality of what was happening. I thought I could escape the ridicule of my classmates by simply not speaking in front of them. I believed I could escape growing up by hiding in medical school for seven years. I escaped from Ireland thinking it would be different in some other country. Whenever the prison walls started to close in, I began plotting my escape.

Unfortunately, I viewed my relationships the same way. The walls closing in. This is not me. I'm trapped. Trapped in a nightmare. Let me out. But who had the key? Who kept the trap shut? Who kept her mouth closed? Who refused to speak? Who kept her locked away? Who was inside?

My choice of medicine wasn't solely determined by the length of the college course, which is often the reason I cite. It was definitely a compelling consideration, and high up on my list of pros and cons, but it wasn't the only reason. Maybe it even gave me an opportunity to hide my more altruistic notions, while discomfiting my parents and teachers. Besides, my two best friends were going. They'd surely help me to survive the duration. I always had a desire to be helpful and knew that doctors did a lot of good in the world. I'd even toyed with the idea of becoming a vet. My love of Marcus Welby MD, and my fascination with the story of Marie Curie clinched it in medicine's favour.

While others were concerned that communication with patients would be difficult, I didn't consider it a problem. That detail was too far in the future to be a concern now. Surely my 'problem' would be resolved by then? I also believed listening was very important. I wanted to listen to others. Listening was so much easier than speaking. No one had listened to me (or seemed to have the patience to listen), and that was the start of a lot of the anxiety for me – the not wanting to waste people's time as they waited for me to say what I wanted to say!

I was a keen listener. I was patient. I noticed how little people actually listened to each other. People were so keen to get their own voice heard and their own opinions expressed and understood, they seemed to have little interest in listening to, or understanding, the opinions, views and experiences of others. I was genuinely interested in hearing what others had to say. First, I was fascinated at how easy fluency seemed to be for everyone else. I watched how they spoke, how the words just flowed out of their mouths, like water. I just asked the questions. There was no need for me to say more. They'd say what needed to be said, and even say what I wanted them to say, eventually. There was no need for me to add my voice to the noise and, anyway, who would've the patience to listen? Silence was easier, to spare everyone's embarrassment, not just my own.

Soon. Soon. I'd be able to say what I wanted to say. Soon. Maybe speaking would be as easy as listening.

Sometimes, listening was difficult. There were those I silently judged and criticised for their ignorance, or misunderstanding, or stupidity. There were those whom I resented because of the ease at which they communicated, yet they said nothing helpful. My listening slowly developed a certain flavour of dissatisfaction, complaint, righteousness. I started to become cynical. Sometimes I despaired. All these people who spoke so easily and all they uttered was nonsense.

I said nothing. I had nothing to say, to contribute, to share. No one knew me. I was nobody. The noise in my head got louder and louder. I was so consumed with hiding to protect myself that I became for myself a coward, cowering in the shadows of my own life. I buried myself in my books, studies, work and travels, trying to avoid and ignore the gnawing reality of my half-lived life.

Looking back, it was a blessing I became a doctor. It was simply the only way open to me to express my compassion for the suffering of others, and my desire to use the gift of my brain and my hands to do the work my voice couldn't do: to relieve the pain, heal the suffering, make the world better, one person at a time.

Over the years, I came to understand that so much of disease (and human suffering) is caused by unhappiness. Most of us have had our young hearts broken, and we numb ourselves to the pain. We pretend we don't care. We hide our broken hearts. And a lot of our unhappiness in life is a result of our failure to communicate the love that is in our heart, out of a fear of being misunderstood, rejected, or hurt. This lack of authentic self-expression leads many people in a downward spiral towards depression. To relieve the stress of everyday life, to express (or suppress) what they cannot express in sobriety, many turn to alcohol, drugs, food and other self-destructive or unhealthy behaviour to find solace. This behaviour eventually leads the patient to the doctor's door. Perhaps, if we could each understand the source of our hurt or suffering, with kindness and compassion, we could help each other heal that little bit easier and reduce the burden of dis-ease in the world.

CHAPTER 3

Hiding the Pain

"The only real prison is fear, and the only real freedom is freedom from fear" – **Aung San Suu Khi**

In my 'day job' as an anaesthetist for 20 years, I would put people to sleep. Since I retired, I'm now in the business of waking people up! Our company, Get Up and Go Publications Ltd, produces the inspirational and motivational Get Up and Go diaries and journals. I left the world of disease and drugs, seeking another way to relieve pain and suffering, and entered the world of wisdom and words to bring comfort and ease.

Why did I choose anaesthesia as a speciality?

Surely it was strange that I ended up in a career that involved putting tubes down people's throats! Is there a "divinity that shapes our ends, Rough-hew them how we will" (*Hamlet*, Shakespeare)? Perhaps it was karma that my own suffering was mirrored so many years later in a career that called for a similar action to facilitate the relief of suffering in others. Or was I simply reliving my own trauma – subconsciously hoping to wake up from the nightmare and the suffering would all be over – as I induced silent sleep, over and over and over again? While I tirelessly called out, "wake up, wake up, wake up – the operation is over", I stubbornly remained asleep.

Anaesthesia was fascinating. I was smart. I loved learning. I understood complicated things. Yet, this was a mysterious area of medicine that confounded me. And it also required practical manual dexterity skills, which I prided myself in. And it suited my personality. Everything happened quickly. There was no chance of boredom – ever!

Despite all my years of undergraduate textbook learning, postgraduate education, training courses, exams and degrees, I can safely say each anaesthetic occurred as a miracle and a mystery. I saw myself as some sort of magician. I'll admit now I don't fully understand how anaesthesia works. Yes, I understand how the drugs work in the brain, i.e. what they do, but my interest is in the mind. What if we knew how to quieten the mind without rendering someone unconscious?

And is the mind quiet when the person is unconscious? I don't know how or why drugs quieten the mind. It simply seems that they can, and they do. What of hypnosis? No drugs there … just words.

We anaesthetise the brain. I know if I give enough anaesthetic drug A, then B (unconsciousness) will happen. I also know if I drink a vast amount of alcohol, I'll pass out! I also know hypnosis works. But that doesn't explain it to me. What happens when we're anaesthetised? Or hypnotised? Or drunk?? Electrical activity in the brain is subdued, and we go to sleep. What about the mind? Where does it go? What of dreams and nightmares??

As an anaesthetist, the most common questions I'd get from a patient about to undergo a surgical procedure would be:

Will I wake up during the operation?

What if I wake up during the operation?

What if I feel pain?

Will I hear people talking while I'm asleep?

What if I hear people talking?

Will I talk while I'm asleep?

Will I wake up at the end?

Of course, my job was to make sure my patient didn't wake up during the operation and did wake up at the end. I had an extensive range of drugs – strong painkillers, sedatives, various anaesthetic medications, relaxants, anti-inflammatory and anti-nausea drugs – all designed and delivered to make sure that no one wakes up during the procedure, that no one suffers awareness, or pain, and each persona wakes up safely, after the surgeon has removed the diseased or damaged part of the body.

However, while the mind is unaware, the body is clearly experiencing something – a fight-or-flight reaction– and a critical role of the anaesthetist is to manage the body's reactions. The body is also reacting to the drugs we've just administered. The heart races or slows, and we control that; breathing increases or decreases, and we control that; the blood pressure rises or falls, so we control that;

if blood is lost, we control that; as fluids shift, we control that; as temperature rises or falls, we control that; if the tendency is for the body is to move, we control that. All this is done while the mind is unaware, because we control the brain.

While this 'insult' is taking place on the body – we're simply preventing any awareness of the suffering. We're numbing the experience, taking away the pain, removing the 'person' from the reality of the situation by controlling the body and anaesthetising the brain for the duration of the procedure.

Was I proud to be an anaesthetist? Absolutely.

Am I very grateful for anaesthesia? Absolutely!

Do I think the world is a better, safer place because of it? Sure it is!

Am I grateful we've something that obliterates the pain or fear of childbirth? Absolutely.

But is there something about the need, desire or acceptance of anaesthesia for surgical interventions, and physical pain, that points to where we don't want to be present to emotional pain; the apparent endless suffering inflicted by human beings on other human beings, including the pain we inflict on ourselves? The pain of rejection, separation, betrayal? This pain is going on all the time, over and over, in our lives, in our world, person to person, nation to nation, generation to generation. When we're numb to the pain we inflict, we can justify being numb to the emotional pain we don't want to experience. When we're numb to our own experience of suffering, we're unconscious to the pain we inflict on others.

Do we truly believe it can all be blotted out – that we can be anaesthetised as we go through life, with drugs, alcohol, hypnosis, work, exercise, denial? Do we delude ourselves into thinking there should be no pain? That we can avoid pain? That pain shouldn't be? That we need to hide it?

Or is there some way we can wake up to the reality of pain, the need to discover the source of pain and then at least try to deal with it effectively? To remove it, and not let it turn into a chronic state of pain and suffering that we need to medicate, numbing ourselves to the impact?

It takes courage to face pain.

It's often the fear of pain that consumes us. Denying our pain, avoiding our pain, resisting our pain, pretending we don't have pain – they all increase the underlying fear and anxiety about the pain, and increase the suffering. Even in the absence of pain, we're consumed with anxiety, and suffer from that. What if I can't bear it? What if I die from the pain?

No one dies from pain.

People die from not dealing with the source of the pain. The pain of appendicitis won't kill you. The pain of surgery won't kill you, but you will surely die if you ignore the pain or do nothing about it or pretend it isn't happening. Then the appendix will rupture, the infection will spread throughout your body, poisoning everything, and you will die.

Fortunately, with physical pain, we're very good at talking about it. It's very acceptable to go to the doctor and have tests and investigations and hopefully find what's at the source of it. Perhaps it needs to be removed, like infected tonsils or an arthritic joint. Perhaps it can be repaired like a broken bone or broken skin, or a broken rib. What about the broken heart or the broken spirit?

Physical pain is alerting us to a danger that might impact our life. We rush to identify, locate, investigate, diagnose and remove or treat, such that we're free to enjoy life again.

What of emotional pain?

This is the pain that robs us of our happiness. Sometimes it accompanies physical pain, with its attendant anxiety. But it's deeper than that. It goes to the source of our suffering. It arises from our unexpressed fears, our hurts, our insecurities, our disappointments. It manifests in depression, and eating disorders, and addictive drinking, or drug taking. But where is it? Where is it located? How can we get to it from where we are?

Animals experience pain, but they don't suffer as we do. They don't have a well-developed emotional component to their behaviour. They seem to have neither memory of pain nor fear of pain. They've no conversation about pain nor agreement that pain is bad, or good, necessary, or anything. They also suffer from the same things as we do: from rejection, loneliness, cruelty, lack of care. Do they suffer from a lack of language?

Human beings are different from other animals. We experience many things when we experience pain, and language adds to the experience. If we've the words to describe our experience, we'll probably say: "It's bad, or terrible, or scary. What's wrong? Why is this happening?" We can progress to: "No one is helping. No one cares. No one loves me. No one understands. I'm on my own. I'm scared."

If we don't have language, we still have these feelings of fear, vulnerability, helplessness or hopelessness. And we don't like that. We feel the need to stop these feelings. We need to control them. We must get to the doctor! We must find out what's wrong! We must get some tablets to numb it or fix it and get better! Perhaps we can't, and perhaps we shouldn't. Perhaps we don't need a doctor. Perhaps we should simply recognise these feelings for what they are – emotions – and normal! Perhaps we just need to express them. Pain is there to alert us to something being 'wrong' and to get us to do something to put it 'right'. We don't cover up physical pain. We know better. We're less confident with admitting to emotional pain. This is where we suffer in silence. It doesn't fit with the image we want to portray to the world. But denying it, pretending it's not there, covering it up, doesn't work. It simply anaesthetises us to ourselves. And when we're numb to our own pain and suffering, we're numb to the pain and suffering of others.

In any area of our lives where we are in pain, suffering or unhappy, we should ask ourselves the following questions:

What is the source of this pain?

The answer is – life. Something has happened.

What is the source of our suffering?

We are. It's our resistance to accepting the reality of life that causes our suffering.

Acceptance of life eliminates suffering. Pain will always be part of our human body experience as we travel the road from birth to death. However, any suffering we endure on this path is primarily down to our own thinking, our words and the way we speak about ourselves and what's happening, to ourselves and others. Pain is inevitable. Suffering is a choice. Accepting this puts us at the source of our own relief.

My interest in suffering and emotional pain led me to consider whether I might pursue a career in psychiatry. Now that was a really interesting area. Not only was I fascinated by the mind, I was truly fascinated by the mind in 'breakdown'. I'd often heard talk of people having 'a nervous breakdown' when I was younger. An aunt had suffered from 'a case of the despondencies'. I wondered about that. As a medical practitioner, listening to the disordered thinking spoken by many of these troubled and distressed patients, disconnected from reality, was fascinating, and sad. This was one area where bizarre thinking was on loudspeaker, for all to hear. In the 'normal' world, we keep that crazy voice well under control – yet over the years I've heard some seemingly very normal people say some very bizarre things. As it happened, during my early training, a kind consultant psychiatrist steered me away with a gentle, "stay away from psychiatry; you'll die there!"

I took his advice. I think I know what he meant. I was too curious about getting to the source of the breakdown, the why of the matter, whereas psychiatry was concerned with diagnosing and treating, to quickly get people back to a socially acceptable way of thinking and behaving.

It's probably not healthy to spend too much time trying to unravel the complexities of the human psyche. Trying to unravel the intricacies of my own mind is a lifetime's work. Perhaps it's for each of us to get clear in our own minds and not depend too much on others to do it for us. We're the only ones who can piece together our living experiences. Our minds get filled up with a whole lot of stuff. Some is useful, valuable and desirable. Other stuff is damaging. Identifying and letting go of the stuff that doesn't serve us is the challenging part. We seem to like holding onto things, even the chains that bind us.

I had one experience that will forever be etched in my memory which highlighted for me the need to get to the source of what makes us who we are. I was a newly appointed Senior House Officer in psychiatry, a relatively junior position, on duty on my first Friday before heading into a bank holiday weekend. I was carrying the emergency bleep, not expecting any emergency and also unsure of what kind of an emergency even presented in psychiatry.

I was only on duty until 5 p.m. Just before 5 p.m., the emergency bleep went off.

I was being called to A+E to assess an elderly woman brought in by her two daughters.

They were all distraught – the two daughters out of obvious concern for their mother, and their mother who looked to me like she was about to explode! She was purple in the face, with wide, staring, bulging eyes and a terrified, panic-stricken look.

The daughters were shouting: "Quick! Quick! She needs emergency ECT!" (Electro Convulsive, or Shock, Therapy).

Having not witnessed such acute distress before, I immediately summoned my senior registrar, and emergency ECT was duly scheduled. My job done, and it now being well past the end of my shift, I handed over the bleep with relief, and went home. But the image haunted me. I'd never seen anyone so clearly terrified in all my life as that woman.

Ever since I'd started in that psychiatry post, I'd been wondering how people broke down the way they did? Why did some people become hyperactive with mania and others catatonic with depression? Why did some people become aggressive and others passive? How did some people's thinking become so bizarre? How did some people become so disconnected from reality? It seemed like people were 'uncontained' at the extremes of human emotion, unrestrained and disinhibited, and had gone outside the norm into this frightening area where people seemed lost, even to themselves, and certainly to their loved ones.

I'd already trained in obstetrics, and believed babies are born 'blank' – beautiful sponges who'd soak up everything in life, to be shaped by their unique experiences, and become people who'd do stuff. I also knew that not everyone turned out good in life. Some people would do great, noble and worthwhile things, and others cruel, hurtful and shameful things. But I never believed any of it was predestined. Every baby was born beautiful, and yet there they were in my psychiatric ward: suffering, broken, lost, alone.

How did they get here? I wanted to know. What happened to the lovely little babies? My curiosity was endless. Asking the patients didn't help – they were beyond my capacity to understand their world. Even though they did their best to communicate, I had no reference point. My task was to listen and look for signs and symptoms we could label with a diagnosis and prescribe the appropriate treatment. This was fundamentally unsatisfying for me. I wanted to get to the bottom of the breakdown, the source of the problem. Surely there must be a reason. *"Don't go there, Eileen – the mind is a bottomless pit".*

On the following Tuesday morning I was doing my early morning rounds before the consultant, so I'd be up to date with all the new admissions over the bank holiday weekend.

I approached this very pleasant elderly lady sitting up comfortably in the bed. I didn't recognise her at first. Then I realised she was the mother who was so distressed and agitated four days earlier. I couldn't believe it. It was my first experience of the 'miracle' of ECT.

I asked her if she remembered coming into A+E with her daughters. "Oh yes," she said, "I was terrified."

"Of what?" I asked.

"It's always the same," she said. "I believe I'm a bomb and if I open my mouth, to speak or even breathe, I'll explode and everything around me will be destroyed."

Wow! The power of belief. And the madness! Where did that belief come from?

I've wondered since – during this journey to discover my own voice and the power of words to create or destroy – as a small child, did she fear saying something? Or did she say something, and all hell broke loose? Did she say something she wasn't supposed to say? Did she see something she wasn't supposed to see? And did that secret just build up inside her over the years, only being released when she was unconscious under anaesthesia for ECT?

My mother had often said: "You are only as sick as your secrets." I think Mum had a point. This unfortunate woman clearly had a secret and clearly, she wasn't well. Now, in her seventies, she had had multiple admissions over the years. It was always the same presentation and the same miraculous result. Was treating the symptoms sufficient? Would an attempt to deal with the cause have prevented a lot of suffering?

I doubt anyone ever got to the bottom of her particular trauma. Perhaps she died with her secrets still inside her.

What would life be like if we didn't feel the need to hide our secrets? What if telling the truth was OK, became the norm, and was encouraged? What if children were trusted to tell the truth and be believed? What if telling the truth was safe? Would we still feel the need to lie to protect ourselves?

Would adults suffer as much if the child they once were, had been listened to and believed, heard and understood, and healed with a kiss? Would that reduce the pain and suffering in the world?

Perhaps your reading of this book will encourage you to get to the source of something that's causing you anxiety, to look deeper into some area of your life where you are less than fully yourself, where you feel you've to hide something. What is that? What could it be? Something you said, did, heard, saw? Something the small child in you didn't quite understand? Discovering the source of your unease gives you the power to deal with it. Perhaps, you couldn't deal with it then, but you can now. Not dealing with it will likely manifest as physical disease.

Being affected by something, especially when we can't see what it is, gives us the experience of powerlessness, making us its victim. We're never the victim when we take action to take back our power. The action takes courage. Sometimes the action is simply the act of looking. It all begins with the willingness.

The intention after every surgical procedure is that the patient wakes up pain-free, comfortable, satisfied and reassured that the source of the problem has been dealt with and they're now on the road to recovery.

Can the same result be achieved by looking for, and dealing with, the source of the emotional pain? Where do we look? The brain? Even if surgery were legitimate, we'd find nothing there. Where could it be, if not the brain? Isn't the brain where everything is stored? Isn't it the brain that is affected by drugs and alcohol, blotting out all our troubles? OK, so if it's not in the brain, surely it's our head? How often are we told, "it's in all in your head"? When we're stressed, our heads ache. When we're reminded of things, we bring them into our mind now. If it's unpleasant, it upsets us. We locate our worries and anxieties in our thoughts, and we locate our thoughts in our heads. It's all in our mind. When we're reminded, we're reminded of the upset.

There's a clue. If it's in our memory – it's from the past. We've no problem with the pleasant stuff. If a memory is pleasant, we delight in it. It's the unpleasant stuff that unnerves us. Why do we forget some things and remember others? What keeps stuff around, especially the unpleasant stuff, in our memories? Something about it is still niggling away, not letting us rest in peace. We love to bring up happy memories, but we try to suppress the unhappy ones. Maybe there's another clue in that.

We must look into our memory to find the source of the upset. It's in there, in the past somewhere. But we know there's nothing in the past. We're not in the past. We can't visit the past. We can't touch it or relive it. It's gone. But something about it is still here, something that got trapped, in language, in some sentence, meaning, decision and we keep it alive in our speaking of it.

And maybe it didn't even happen quite as we remember it. Maybe memory has coloured or distorted or exaggerated or minimised it in some way. Which is why we can't grasp it. Yet it remains a constant reminder of some upset, some hurt, some emotion that got locked in. And what's the point of looking, of 'raking up the past'? Shouldn't we let sleeping dogs lie? Aren't we doing OK? We can't go back there anyway, to fix it or change it. We might as well forget about it.

Somehow, that doesn't seem to work so well. My psychiatry patient is testament to that. Maybe there's another way. Maybe to forget isn't the answer, but to forgive? Maybe we can accept it, make peace with it? We're here now, not there, then. We can accept what happened. We can even forgive ourselves for the part we played. We can change the way we remember it and speak about it. We don't need to suffer. We can let go of the significance we've attached to it. It will then release its grip on us. Therefore, we don't need to punish. We just need to live at ease with the past, in the present, and the way it is, disease free. We can now say something different, so the future seems brighter, lighter, not so weighed down by having to carry the weight of some terrible secret. It worked for me!

In this book, you've an opportunity to be the surgeon in your own operation. You don't need an anaesthetist. The instruments aren't sharp. Words can be blunt, but not harsh. You must become detached from the 'patient' and simply carry out the procedure. You have the knife. You know where the wounds are. You make the cut. Do it with love.

How fortunate that you've me as your guide. I'm your practice patient. I made the cut. I did the digging. Yes, it was painful to expose the depth of my suffering, to dissect the layers, release the adhesions, find the memory. I had much to forgive. And I survived. I emerged, like a butterfly from a cocoon, well on the road to recovery, liberated, like I'd grown wings.

You can use my journey as evidence the operation will be a success. Like any good patient, you do, however, need to trust your doctor.

As a doctor, my promise on taking the Hippocratic Oath is always: Do No Harm.

As the (initially reticent) patient, I promise the procedure was well worth it.

CHAPTER 4

Whose Voice is This Anyway?

"The voice of the intellect is a soft one, but it does not rest until it has gained a hearing" – **Sigmund Freud**

Life is all about taking risks. On the physical side of things, there wasn't much I was afraid of, in terms of my own ability to survive them. I watched others closely. If they could do it, I could do it.

I spent my childhood climbing trees, jumping off walls, roller-skating faster than anyone else, skipping, running. Anything at all that even sniffed of adventure, I wanted to try it. I loved funfairs, with all the music and energy and excitement to add to my experience of joy and freedom: scream, laugh, cry, experience all the emotions, including terror, safely. Wonderful. I still love funfairs to this day, my favourites being Coney Island in New York, Disneyland in California, and Islands of Adventure in Orlando, Florida. I made it my mission to seek out funfairs on all my travels, local or abroad. I can't imagine any other occasion in life where that single experience of fear and excitement is so available and predictable.

I experienced something similar when I did a fundraising parachute jump for Save the Children with the Red Devils – a branch of the British Army – in 1984. This too was an exhilarating experience. I was in freefall, having thrown myself backwards out of the plane at almost 15,000 ft above Aldershot, waiting for instructions to open my parachute, falling. Then being lifted, flying, plain sailing and slowly coming down to land. Then it was all over, bar the story.

Or rafting the rapids on the Zambezi river in Tanzania. Or flying a microlight over Victoria Falls. Or coming through the clouds at dawn as I climb to the top of Kilimanjaro. Or the awe of being on the edge of the Himalayas as the peak of Mount Everest comes into view. Or riding an ostrich, or a runaway horse, or cycling through Ho Chi Minh City in rush hour.

I've had the most extraordinary life. I was someone who always wanted to say "yes". It seems like I said yes to everything but speaking. My mum was a YES person. She loved to say "yes please", "yes thank you", "yes, certainly", "yes, I'd love to", "yes you can", "yes I will", "yes, I'll try". There was rarely a "no", in my memory.

But perhaps I didn't demand much. Maybe I was happy enough with what I had or resigned that I'd never have what I wanted anyway. And I always had enough of everything else. In fact, I was eager to give away what I had, so others could share the joy. I think I learnt the joy of sharing from my mother. She always seemed happy to me: happy to be asked, to receive, to be wanted, to be needed, to contribute, be involved, invited, included.

I shared my new kitten once, with our next-door neighbours. They'd never seen such a tiny creature. They lifted him and examined him and twisted him this way and that, and he broke. I could hear the crack and the cry. I cried too. I had to forgive them. "They didn't understand," Mam had said.

Mostly, Mam said no to herself, rarely to others. But it was silent, so I didn't hear that. It seems she was resigned too.

She told me a story about a school bag once. She loved school. She grew up in a small town with not many shops. One day there appeared in a shop window a beautiful brown leather school bag with a handle and a shining buckle. She really wanted the school bag, but knew they didn't have much money, so she was reluctant to ask her mother. So, the school bag remained in the window. One day, she summoned up the courage to ask her mother if she would buy her the school bag. "OK", she said, "but not now." That was enough. Her mother would buy her the school bag. She was so excited and told her friends about her new school bag. Every time they passed the shop window, she asked if she could buy it that day. "Not now. Later." One day, walking past with her mother, they met her mother's neighbour right outside the shop window. Mam was tugging at her sleeve: "What about today, my school bag?"

"Stop that, child!" her mother said crossly, embarrassed in front of her friend. "It's NOT your school bag, and you aren't getting any school bag. Now, stop annoying me about it!" Mam was devastated. There was no mistaking from her mother's tone that there would be no school bag: not now, not today, not ever.

The message to her was don't be greedy, don't want – you should be happy with what you have.

So, I think she stopped wanting that day, and decided to be happy with what she got.

I think I inherited a little bit of that too, and it's not such a bad thing.

So, where did I get my spirit of adventure? Certainly not from my dad, who was ultra-cautious, responsible, thoughtful, conservative. No, Mam was definitely the culprit.

Thank you, Mam, for my spirit of adventure. Thank you for being the person who encouraged me to say "yes" in life.

I only realised this quality about her in later years, when I discovered that not only was she my mother, but a real person with a real life before me.

She told me that when she was seventeen, she had a secret boyfriend. I wasn't surprised as, in some of her early photos, the ones she hadn't defaced with a pencil, she was extraordinarily beautiful.

She didn't mention if this was approved or not, but as it was Catholic Ireland in the early 1940s, I gathered it was most likely frowned upon.

Anyway, he was leaving to work in Donegal, which was like going to America in those days. She wanted to give him a present – a hairbrush and comb set she'd seen in the chemist's window in a neighbouring town. It was mid-winter and snowing and she hadn't much money, but she sneaked out, took her bicycle and cycled seventeen miles in the snow and the dark to get to the shop she knew would be open until late and bought the present. She cycled home, exhilarated, proud and happy she got the gift for him before he left.

I heard no more about him. What she recalled was the freedom, the feeling of accomplishment, the spirit of adventure, of being daring, breaking the rules, being alive. Being cold and wet and a little scared, on purpose. On a mission, her mission, an adult mission. A girlfriend buying a special gift for her boyfriend. Whether he ever remembered the gift, she certainly remembered the journey.

I had my first taste of freedom and adventure when I went to the Gaeltacht when I was fifteen. I climbed out of the window at 3 a.m. and went to meet a boy I'd met at the Irish dancing evening. I loved the ceílí. I had won medals for Irish dancing. He was from Cork and he was eighteen. I was smitten. We were so innocent. We sat at the edge of the lake, on a small wall, holding hands, watching the sun come up. The lake was like glass, and two swans came in to land on the water, gliding silently till they came to float in the middle of the lake, the ripples spreading out behind them like huge, waving wings. I'd never seen anything so beautiful in my life. I think I fell in love with the world that night. Whatever, about the boy! Like Mam, what I experienced was the spirit of adventure, of being daring, breaking the rules, being alive, being cold and a little bit scared, a 'girlfriend' sitting on a wall with her first 'boyfriend' – in blissful silence.

A few years later, while still a medical student, I was working for the summer in a restaurant kitchen in Oberstdorf, Germany. My friend was working in the Rappenseehuette, a mountain lodge used by trekkers walking the high hills. I thought it might be nice to visit her on my day off. The villagers were moving 3,000 cows to the higher pastures and I was to travel with them. My German wasn't very good, but they got the idea of what I wanted to do. The day started at 4 a.m. We reached the pastures around noon. Someone then pointed to a small path and said – go that way. So I went. It was a beautiful day. I wore a light green skirt and a flowery cotton tee shirt and sandals. No one told me otherwise. And so I walked, and walked, and climbed, and climbed, for hours, until I came to the snow line. And still I walked. Here I was, twenty-two years old, alone, in the Alps.

And I sang at the top of my voice: "The hills are alive with the sound of music."

I arrived as night fell. I was tired, but I think I was the happiest person in the world. I'd travelled one of the most magical and liberating journeys of my entire life. The entire experience was one of pure joy and freedom. There was nothing and no one to fear. I was on a path. I was on an adventure. I was alive.

The modest wooden lodge was delightful. Breda was relieved to see me, almost sixteen hours after I'd set off that morning.

After dinner, we sat by the window looking into the deep blackness. Suddenly, there was a lightning storm. With each flash of lightning, the entire range of white, alpine peaks were illuminated for a split second by the piercing white light. Awesome. I was moved to tears by the power and beauty of it all.

The journey down was different. I thought better of the long walk; it was a lot further away than I'd expected. The alternative was a type of homemade cable car, used for transporting supplies. It looked safe enough. There was another girl game enough to give it a go, so we sat in the 'car'. They gave us an umbrella each and covered our laps with a tarpaulin, and off we sailed, down the mountain. Not quite a rollercoaster but equally exhilarating. It didn't go straight down, but sort of lurched between the posts just skimming the tops of the trees. I didn't care. It was an almighty adventure and I was hooked. If this was what life was about, I was playing. I was fearless – or so I believed.

*****

My dear, devoted dad. Steady, dependable, reliable, conservative, safe, cautious, responsible, kind, generous, thoughtful, friendly, who stayed in the same job for forty-seven years so we could have an education and holidays and books and clothes: whatever we needed, whenever we needed it.

However, I didn't see this person when I was growing up: the person who adored my mother, idolised his children, who was grateful for his life, who loved religion and politics and history and poetry and geography and education and brought the world to our kitchen table.

Instead, I saw an old man (too old) with white hair and blue eyes, who smoked too much, coughed a lot, always ate the same food, and read the same newspaper. In a word: boring. And he'd failed to protect me when I needed him most. I looked at him through judgemental and unforgiving eyes, and I took my love away from him too. He never took his love away. His only daughter: his beautiful, blonde, freckled, spirited firebrand. How could he not love me!

Fortunately, I 'met' my dad before he died. I 'grew up' during his last few years, as his health failed. This occurred as a result of a row I had with my younger brother. He articulated what I felt but didn't admit – that Dad had failed me – and I couldn't be with the truth of that. In hearing myself speak during that argument, I realised how I was behaving toward him, how I judged him, and the injustice of that, and resolved to make amends. I could stop punishing him for what I thought he'd done that had failed me.

Only after that realisation could I clearly see him for who he was and acknowledge him for being such a great father to me. He was my role model for a just world, a christian world (with a small c), a forgiving world. His loyalty, integrity, pride and devotion, his generosity, willingness to serve, love for education, desire for peaceful resolution to conflict ("blessed are the peacemakers"), delight in the simple things and his passion for fairness were his gifts to me. They had come from his own father, whom he never met, but who in giving life to my father, and dying for the freedom of his country, miraculously gave me meaning for mine. "It's the chains of the past that bind us."

And I made my peace with him. He'd done the best he could.

Dad never wanted me to be a doctor. There were no doctors ever in our family. My mother had been a nurse until she married. Dad had a friend who was a doctor and he thought it was a thankless life, and I wouldn't be happy. He just wanted me to be happy, and healthy.

He knew first-hand the value of health. Having suffered with TB as a young man, he spent three years in hospital, never expecting to go home again, watching too many of his friends leave in coffins. Luckily, he was given an opportunity to take part in the country's first Streptomycin drug trial at thirty-three years of age, and willingly accepted. A prior painful thoracoplasty, leaving him functionally with only one lung, had failed to cure him. Miraculously, he responded to the treatment, and left hospital a happy man.

My mother had been his nurse. They met again while getting on/off a bus not long after his release, and the rest is history. They married in 1957.

His father, my grandfather, Seán Mac Caoilte, wasn't so lucky. He died of TB aged thirty-six in October 1922, less than three months after my dad was born (Dad was always proud of the fact he was born in the same year as the Irish Free State). He had already buried two of his other children, Dad's older brothers, aged two and eight, both on the same day.

Seán was a journalist and had been involved in politics as a member of the old Sinn Fein. He was a pro-treaty supporter of Michael Collins, believing negotiation was the only way to achieve freedom, independence and peace in Ireland. He was sent to the US to speak on this subject to get support for the Treaty, at large open-air rallies. Unfortunately, the political landscape had changed during the six months he was away, and on his return, he was arrested and interned in Arbour Hill, where he contracted TB. On his release from prison, he obviously brought the infection with him and, with no immunity, and no treatment, all three succumbed to the disease. My Dad, eight weeks old at the time, survived and only became ill in his late twenties, fortunately living long enough with the disease for a cure to be found.

Dad was immensely proud of his father and the role in played in his country's history, even though he never actually met him. I never heard a bitter word uttered against the British or the people who interned his father or those who caused his mother so much grief and hardship after her husband's death. He simply said we must forgive. We cannot carry a burden of resentment or regret through life. That will only eat away at our soul. It will rob us of our enjoyment, our own happiness in our own lives. We must be peaceful in our own hearts. We must be free from hate and thoughts of revenge.

Before Seán's untimely death at 38 years old, he'd been a Dublin City Councillor and was tipped to be the next Lord Mayor. He was an author, a playwright, a journalist, a dancer, a passionate Gaelgóir (one who loves Irish culture and language) and a powerful advocate for justice, peace and freedom. I would love to have known him.

At 33, Dad had another shot at life, one he didn't expect. He was grateful for the gift. He was grateful he could live in good health in a free and peaceful country, and to his father for dying for that. We must all play our part.

There was considerable speculation or hope that someone in our family might have followed my grandfather into politics; not to die for Ireland, but to stand up for it, this country we loved and were so proud of. Ireland had taken its rightful place among the nations of the world, yet we couldn't reconcile the grievances on our own divided island. Somewhere there was a glimmer of hope that perhaps I, with my idealistic nature, passionate sense of justice, and forthright and argumentative spirit, could be that person.

Of course, with my speech impediment, this never occurred as even remotely possible to me, nor was it even in the realm of desire, but it seems for many years my parents, especially my mother, still saw some future for me in politics or law or journalism or education. She could never understand why I chose medicine! She had never been impressed with my bedside manner and remarked how I would have made a terrible nurse.

I have always been passionate about health and well-being, as it's vital that people are healthy and free to enjoy life on this wonderful planet of ours, in peace! I live life such that others can live too. I believe life should be worth living and dying for. Something has to be. We're all going to die anyway. It's challenging to think we can live a life worth dying for. I'm sure I'm here for something. Perhaps there's something in our family narrative that is yet to be told. Perhaps it's up to me to invent a personal narrative. Maybe there's a future not yet written that will allow some more of the dots to be joined backwards. Maybe

I can use my voice to tell another story. Maybe I'm here to give it purpose. My purpose. A meaning and purpose worthy of my life.

My grandfather is now dead and silent as the grave. As is my father. I'll die one day too. What do I want to leave after me? What do I want to do or say that will show I was here, that I lived, had a voice, that what I said mattered, that I mattered, that my life made a difference?

If I don't speak, don't stand for something, speak up for something, act in service of some larger purpose, then what am I doing? Living, yes, or simply existing, waiting for life to be over, so I can Rest In Peace? My life is worth more than that. My life is a book of which I'm the author. Everyone's life is a book, with the pages constantly turning; blank pages of tomorrow gradually being filled with happenings, experiences, stories that too soon become yesterday. It's up to each of us to live such that our book is a true memoire, memorable in that the telling of it might provide a glimpse of what could be possible to enrich the life of another.

The fact I didn't find my ultimate career satisfaction in anaesthesia or even in medicine is testament to the fact my natural self-expression was indeed thwarted, leaving me upset and unfulfilled for most of my life, searching for that elusive something that would have it all make sense. Incredibly, I was enlightened by my own words.

*****

I consider myself extremely lucky that I was presented with the opportunity to follow a passion that led to a new career as an 'entrepreneur'. I'd been involved in compiling The Irish Get Up and Go Diary, alongside my half-time anaesthesia position, for almost ten years, before I took early retirement from the health service. I then took the brave step of growing the publishing company as a means of creating more products that would inspire and motivate more people, so they could inspire and empower themselves to live their best one-and-only life, one great day at a time. This was what truly lit me up and, with a new level of confidence and courage that came from knowing I was now on the right path, allowed me to pursue it with enthusiasm.

For my own desire for new knowledge and inspiration I continued with my newly discovered education in 'wisdom'. Humanity is what particularly interested me and, as I educated myself about my own humanity and my own human nature, I questioned why we do what we do – even when it doesn't serve us.

As I continued to explore my own life, and coupled with my own experience of the wider world, I shared the insights and lessons learnt to provide some benefit for others. For me, it all came down to words.

When I found my voice, and the courage to speak up and say what I wanted to say, it turned my world on its head. Having found the courage to look back on my life and see where I'd made crucial decisions that impacted my life and damaged my relationships, then clear it up with those people, such that we could now move forward, was hugely liberating for me. I felt as though the chains of my past were finally being broken and I was now free to be my true self in the world, living the life I wanted to live. I was no longer pretending to be happy, hiding myself away, working hard and secretly hoping for some miracle. It's never too late to make amends.

When I started on this journey of enquiry into who I was and how come I wound up being 'me' in the world, and who was this 'me' anyway that I referred to as 'I'. I realised I wasn't alone in this quest.

Many people had been on this journey before me. Over the centuries, philosophers and theologians and writers and scientists and artists and humanitarians and psychologists and activists of all sorts have grappled with this conundrum – this eternal question of 'Who am I? Why am I here? What is it all for?'

Numerous words have been spoken and written over millennia, with glimpses of universal realisations and truisms and constants. This is what fascinated me: the words, sentiments, emotions, thoughts, phrases, poetry, sentences, experiences, lives. They were now trapped on the pages, in the explanations, musings, memories, interpretations, opinions, views, stories, facts, fiction, contradictions, revisions, recollections, fantasies. All the words ever written, that had ever made a difference for mankind. Truths, lies, opinions, stories; what were they all for if not to enlighten, contribute, educate and to stir people to action?

Books. Words. Words on a page – waiting to be liberated, or to liberate.

The Gospel of John begins with: "In the beginning was the Word, and the Word was with God, and the Word was God". Wow! What a statement. Even though I'd heard it read out in church over the years, without giving it any attention, I heard it with a new and profound awareness.

As human beings we have language – we can create words and sentences and we can act on those sentences. The most powerful people in history have harnessed the power of words to achieve great things. In fact, nothing exists in our man-made world that didn't have its origin in a word, a thought, in the mind of a human being.

And yet most of the time we use our words with abandon. We throw them out carelessly, indiscriminately, thoughtlessly, irresponsibly, as if they were inconsequential. We're not mindful of where they might land, oblivious to the fact that when they land in the listening ears of young children, they can cause untold harm. By the time we reach adulthood, we've generally closed our ears – to protect ourselves from careless words that have hurt and betrayed us. Yet we still speak from the upset and anger of small children, not getting what we want. We put the most powerful tool (or weapon) in the world into the mouths of babes – and it came without instruction.

So, from my early prison of self-imposed silence, I now find myself revelling in the awesome world of words, and the power of words to create worlds, both wanted and unwanted.

From a career involving anaesthetising people and putting tubes down their throats so they can be connected to a breathing machine in order to stay alive, I'm now inhabiting the world of words and how words can inspire people to live or, with equanimity, cause disconnection and destroy the will to live. We're all responsible for what comes out of our mouths, and it behoves us to be mindful of the awesome power our words have and the dangerous weapon they can be. The pen is, indeed, mightier than the sword.

In creating diaries and journals that will inspire and motivate people to live empowered lives, I gather some of the most memorable words that resonate with me as 'true': wise words spoken fifty, a hundred, maybe hundreds of years before, by people who, by their words, continue to inform, influence, inspire and motivate people to this day. And they're all the same, ordinary words spoken daily by ordinary people all over the world.

What did that say about people?

We like to communicate. We need to communicate. We want to communicate.

That words matter.

Our words matter.

If we speak with an intention, words are the most powerful force on the planet.

We say "talk is cheap" – we don't want to admit that maybe we cheapen talk, when we say things that aren't true, when we practise to deceive, when we waste our precious breath on banal commentary that makes no difference.

And I knew all about that. I knew what it was like to live like that. I had a voice that lied. I lied. I asked for an apple when I wanted a packet of crisps. I asked to get off the bus in Santry when I wanted to get off in Beaumont. I said no when I wanted to say yes.

Whose was this voice that sabotaged most of my life?

Yes, of course it was mine, but I didn't want it. I wanted another voice. I wanted a voice that said what I wanted it to say. But it didn't. It stuttered and stammered and stopped and got excited and frustrated and upset. And tumbled out in "ratttttatttaattt" or "bbbbbbbbbbbbbrrrnnrr" or "mmmmmbbb" or "mmmm" or "Dddidddddbdnntdddddid" or "bubububuuuubbbbbbtttt" or "cccccccudccccud" or "ccaaaccaaa" or "Sttsstttttssttt". To the point of exhaustion, of myself and anyone listening.

You get the picture. Betrayed by my own voice. So, I stopped. What I had to say probably wasn't important anyway. Why bother? Nobody was interested. Forget about it.

And I became an anaesthetist. And anaesthetised people put tubes down their throats. How bizarre it seemed, when I finally got to look at it, that my life had turned out the way it did. Back where it all started, with tubes down throats.

Words have awesome power both to create and destroy. We can create a new future by saying "I do" and we can kill off a possibility with a "No thank you". Even a six-year-old can kill off her love for her mother with: "Get away from me. I hate you."

Scary, huh?

CHAPTER 5

The Struggle to Let Go

"The cave you fear to enter holds the treasure you seek" –
Joseph Campbell

In 2001, a colleague invited me to attend a personal development seminar, and I accepted.

Why not? The timing was right. My marriage had just ended, which had catapulted me to an unwelcome crossroads, and I didn't know what to do next. I'd reached what seemed like that 'point'. The proverbial end of the line, point zero; all of my strategies were exhausted. I wasn't where I'd expected to be in my life by now, and it wasn't looking like I'd ever get there. I looked into the future and it looked bleak. I didn't even know how my life had got to this point; I just knew I didn't want it any more.

This wasn't supposed to happen to me. I was supposed to be happily married, with a family and a great career. Now I was planning a divorce and I had no children. My career was in limbo. There was no real purpose or direction in my life. I was getting older. My friends were busy with children and grandchildren. I was working long hours in a job I enjoyed but, somehow, it wasn't fulfilling me. I wasn't jumping out of bed in the morning with excitement. I was more getting through the week until the weekend, still dreading the 'on-call', and getting through the month for the next pay cheque, and getting through the year for the holiday I badly needed. I'd waited for my perfect life to happen and was still waiting – and now losing hope. The life I had wasn't the life I'd wanted. It seemed like I went to sleep on a train a long time ago and woke up in a foreign country.

Where was I? How did I get here? What had happened to me? Where did my life go?

I was tired. I still had lots of dreams, but that was all they were. Where did I want to live? What did I really want to do? What kind of life did I really want to have? Who did I really want to be now that I was no longer someone's wife?

But did I really want to look at my life? I had a choice here. I could say no and carry on down that scary, lonely road and hope for the best. Or say yes and...

All I knew was I didn't want the life I had. I wanted more. When I applied to do the seminar, I wrote on the form, in tiny writing, in pencil, by way of answer to the question 'What do you want to get from the seminar?' – "I don't want to live a little life."

So, there I was, in a public forum, listening while total strangers shared about their lives in honest, real and meaningful conversations. On the surface, it seemed like they were all people just like me: living busy lives, outwardly successful and not quite knowing why they/we were here. The more I listened, the more I felt an uneasy discomfort, a resistance, a growing awareness: "This is it. This is my life. No! This can't be it! This can't be all there is! There must be more!" And I wanted more.

And I was stuck.

It was all very well for these people who could go to the microphone, who could express themselves, who could ask for what they wanted.

I couldn't do that.

I needed to explain my case...

Later that evening – at the end of a long session – I approached the trainer and waited in line for my turn...

Within seconds, I was desperately trying to explain my predicament: why I was different, why my circumstances were "special", why I couldn't go to the microphone. I was upset. I was crying. I needed this person who was leading the seminar to understand why I couldn't speak like other people.

"Really? Says who?"

"I do."

"Well, stop saying that. And stop crying!"

"What?"

"Stop crying."

"I can't – I'm upset."

"You won't."

"I can't (sobbing)."

"You won't."

"I can't..."

"You won't."

"I will... (tears falling)"

"Then stop..."

"I can't... (calming ... I was beginning to hear the lie)"

"You won't."

"I will (calm)."

"Good. When?"

The chasm opened up. That was the question that changed my life. That question, leading to that split second of reflection, of choice. I was being challenged to consider a new view, from a different place

I resisted. I wanted to argue for my view. I had a lifetime of evidence and a life to prove it. I wasn't letting it go. I couldn't let it go, could I? After all this time?

He looked at me ... waiting.

The chasm seemed like an eternity.

I looked deeper. Was my "cannot" actually a "will not" – a wilful refusal to try?

Trying had proven an abysmal failure. By thirteen, it seemed I'd tried and tried for years. I was exhausted. I'd failed. I was done trying. I knew if I kept trying, I'd fail forever. I gave up. I simply didn't have the courage. I thought I could find another way to express myself or find another person to express for me. I thought I'd manage. I thought I could make it work. I thought I'd show them. I thought no one need ever know how much of a coward I was. I was wrong. My life was testimony to that.

I'd stopped saying anything real, and I stopped listening to others. What they were saying wasn't real either. We were all silent about the things that mattered. Silence, they say, is the voice of complicity.

But my silence was deliberate. It was the ultimate punishment for the ultimate suffering. "I can't and don't ask me.". "I won't and you can't make me.". "Leave me alone" – the wilful refusal and simple command against which there was no argument.

I failed to be happy, and those who loved me would fail also. If I was suffering, they would suffer also. This was to be their punishment. I'd succeed in that.

Who was this person? This alien? This person who'd taken over my life – and gone on the path of revenge to silence me.

Having lived a lie, so perfectly, had I tricked myself out of my own life?

The realisation was enormous. The moment had come. This was my moment... The moment my "I can't" was challenged by "you won't", a door opened for me.

What if my "I can't" was simply "I won't"?

I could find out. I had a choice. I could change my "I won't" to "I will". I could trust. I was trapped, but I could be free. Now. All it would take was changing my "no" to a "yes". My future in three letters, one word.

The question was: "When?" My when was never.

When would I let go of the story – the "I can't" – and the life and drama that went with it? I could change "never" to "now".

That was the dilemma...

Silence.

The chasm...

The universe was making a request.

And I was silent.

Here was an invitation to let go of who I thought I was and create myself as the person I wanted to be, had always wanted to be. The person free from the trap of who I thought I was. The person I wound up being by accident, free to be anything I wanted: a writer, speaker, an inspiring voice, a courageous leader.

It sounded wonderful – and terrifying!

I wouldn't have to die with my music still inside me – but what music was it?

Now I had a clear choice. Continue with the lie or let it go and let the truth come out?

My head was going crazy. If I let go of the lie, who was I? Who was I if I wasn't the liar? Who was I without my story: the lie (life) I'd lived? What was the truth for me? If I was not the liar, then I was the liar. If 'not' was the lie, then I could let go of the 'not' and be the liar. That was the truth. I could let go of the cannot and be the can.

I was swimming through mud. My brain was a thick fog of confusion.

My mind began to clear, as the truth emerged through the fog. It was like I could now see the water I swam in. I could let go of the "will not" and be the will. I could let go of the "not now" and be it, now. I'd be free. All it would take was letting go of the "not".

There's no "no/not" in life. There's only 'no/not' in language. The daffodil doesn't say: "I'll not flower today." There's no "not now", there's only now. There's no "not" anywhere. There's no 'nothing'; there's only something or the absence of something. There's no "no" in the universe. We made up the "no" when we discovered language. We needed something to explain the nothing. We said, "no thing". Like no sun could explain the darkness. Or no smile could explain the sadness.

So, I could free myself now. All it would take was the willingness. Was I willing? Willing to change "no" and "not" to "yes"?

My future in three letters. To let go of another small three letter word: "not."

Could I?

I can "not"?

I can?

Two futures.

One, more of the past. MY past. A "no", "not now": a refusal, an inability, an unwillingness.

The other new, unknown. My future. A "yes": an acceptance, a willingness to discover something new.

It all rested on my willingness to let go of one small word, screaming silently in my head, and to let another fall out of my mouth. The one that would be heard.

The question was: "When?"

My answer: "Now!"

Yes, I'd got myself into the perfect place. And I was now here, after all these years, standing at a microphone, in front of 150 people, shaking! Yes, it had taken me three days: three days of listening and arguing with the 'voice in my head' that told me I should just go home!

They were all waiting for me to say something. They were willing me to say something. I knew "I can't" would be a lie. I was scared my voice would betray me, that the words would get stuck. But I had given my word. I had said "I will." So, there I was, willing. This was my leap of faith, my daring act, my chance. My chance to find out what it was I was so scared of. I knew, simply by just standing there, willing, this was already a turning point in my life. This was my chance, my time, now or never. My once-in-a-lifetime opportunity. Terrified, I took it.

"Hello."

I spoke clearly. I heard my voice reverberating around the room. I was astounded at how even and clear it was. Again, I said "Hello", and smiled at the front row.

"My name is Eileen Forrestal." People smiled up at me, listening. "I just want to thank all of you who came to the microphone before me. I couldn't have got here without your encouragement."

There was suddenly nothing to be scared of.

"And now, I want to forgive myself for staying silent, in my chair, for so long. Thank you again, I love you all."

I sat down. Wow. No one gasped. No one laughed. No one looked up in horror. I'd done the very thing that had stopped me my whole life. I'd felt the fear and did it anyway. I'd opened my mouth and let the words fall out. They were simple. They were honest. No drama. The only thing in the world I thought I could never do. Stand up, speak up, and say what I wanted to say. To 150 people! For me. I risked it. It came out right first time. I, and everyone else, had heard my voice, heard me speaking. Now I was out, now I was free. Now I was out of the trap. Suddenly I was free of all of it. I had a say in the matter. This was the most empowering and liberating thing imaginable. The spell had been broken and I'd broken it. I'd broken it with my own words. My words had set me free from the sentence my own words had trapped me in, almost thirty years earlier.

I was reeling with a discovery about the simplicity and comic-tragedy of my life. Was it just me, or was this part of the human condition: the gift and the treachery of language, of what we give voice to, silent or otherwise? I'd conditioned myself. I'd imprisoned myself. I'd now liberated myself. I was released, as a prisoner is released from a life sentence, exhilarated and terrified at the same time.

Now I could say anything, and I wanted it to always be the truth for me. I was done with the lies, excuses, reasons. The truth was simple. The words I spoke were the simple truth: they were honest, no drama, no story, no explanations. My words had said exactly what I wanted them to say. The truth was easy. It was clear. It was straight. It was powerful. The one thing in the world I thought I could never do, simply because I was too scared to try, and to tell the truth about that, about how scared I was, was all it took. Now the truth was out, I was out. I was free. I listened to my heartbeat – I was calm. The truth had set me free. Free at last. Free to be me. I was home and at peace.

The words we use and don't use are access and the barriers to everything.

Now I was ready to have the conversation of my life, and to tell the truth to the only person who mattered. My mother.

That was it! Of course I could. I could, all along. I just didn't.

I could own the truth. The truth of who I was, in my heart.

Looking back, I can still remember my heart racing before I braced the stage that evening. Where was the courage? It had to be there, in my heart – right there, pounding as if forcing itself through my ribcage. Where else could it be? Could it have been out there – in the room where I was being invited to speak – into the generous listening of others, who had the courage to share before me?

I was now aware of the new power I had – the power of my word. I also had a new realisation – my word as myself. I could say anything now and it would be true to myself. I could never again separate myself from my word. I am who I say I am right now. The author of my own story. I could have my life go the way I said: consciously, deliberately, intentionally. I'd created my life by default with a lie. What could I create with the truth? What I said now could really matter.

I was out. The truth had set me free. What would I do with the freedom? That was now there to be discovered.

The challenge was to stay out: to keep speaking the truth, my truth, the truth for me. Not everyone wants to hear the truth, and not everyone hears the truth in the same way. There are many people hiding out in life, for safety, afraid to be seen. Not everyone wants to come out as who they are. Most of us don't even know who we are. We just know who we wound up being. Many of us are afraid of who we think we are, or fear we're not. Many of us are afraid to contemplate who we think we could have been, or should have been.

The beauty of coming clean, is the discovery that we're, in fact, a moment-by-moment creation, as fluid as what comes out of our mouths. We're not carved in stone. We are the stone, and the chisel, and the hand. We're as much actors on a stage as anyone who gets paid huge sums of money in Hollywood. We're the actor, the director and the scriptwriter. We're the singer and the songwriter. We choose the song.

The awesome responsibility of this realisation hit me between the eyes. I was the sole owner of my own life. All of it. Now what? With my new-found courage I was ready to embark on a new and exciting adventure – my big life.

Once I'd started, I had to keep going. I was curious myself as to what was going to come out of my own mouth, as I created this new chapter of my life with my new courage and my new freedom with words. I could say anything, and honour what I said. Creating the future from this place, this new beginning, this blank sheet, was no small thing. In fact, its vastness was terrifying.

I decided to start with a simple "I love you." That was the simple truth. My love was out. I was out. My self was free to be expressed. There wasn't anything to hide.

But first I had to say it to my mother – and the truth of those words was the most liberating truth of all.

CHAPTER 6

Trust and Betrayal

"This above all: to thine own self be true. And it must
follow, as the night the day, thou canst not then be false to
any man" – **William Shakespeare, Hamlet**

I'd spent my entire life running away from my mother or, more accurately, running away from her love. In her world, I could do no wrong. I was her only daughter: her beautiful, smart, clever, funny, charming daughter. Only that wasn't how I saw myself – with my split ends, freckles, crooked teeth – and the wretched stammer.

Mam knew all my friends, and all about school. She listened patiently over the years to every complaint and frustration I had with school, teachers, church, priests, politics, the 'system', the world, the law, my studies, career, tutors. Everyone and everything was a source of complaint: the world should not be this way; people should not do what they do; why could people not just do the right thing? Why was there so much injustice, unfairness, poverty, hunger, corruption, disease, pain, loneliness and suffering? She listened patiently, always in agreement. We talked over endless cups of tea into many nights by the kitchen fire.

But something was missing. I kept her firmly outside my 'life' – my inner, personal life, my worries, dreams, fears. She would occasionally ask about boyfriends, with that sweet, curious smile, hoping maybe I'd share a daughter-mother bonding moment. No way! Number one: how could I ever have a boyfriend? Didn't she KNOW about the damned stammer? 'I can't even speak properly. Who would want ME?' And anyway, even if I had, it was none of her business. I punished her by withholding my love, and we both suffered for that.

If she wanted to see some happiness for me, I was determined to prove her wrong. I couldn't and wouldn't be happy. And I'd PROVE it to her. How could anyone be happy with me when I was so unhappy with myself? How could anyone know me when I was such a stranger to myself?

So we discussed the world, and life, and everything I knew about and could understand ... until it came close to home. My hair, eating habits, clothes, posture, my voice. "That hairstyle doesn't suit you", "that colour isn't so good on you", "you really shouldn't be smoking" and, of course, the usual "slow down, and speak properly!"

Then my reaction was swift – and ruthless. A silent: "Go away, I hate you." I would leave, in a temper, annoyed and upset. Why would she not accept me as I am? It was MY hair and I'd wear it the way I wanted to. It was my 'style'; I'd wear what I liked! Why could she not accept me as I was? And I CANNOT speak properly!

I didn't bother to enquire into why I behaved that way. I just had my 'reasons' and I was justified, and "she should know better" by now! There was too much juice to be extracted from the story.

She'd always loved me. She only ever wanted the best for me. She knew me better than I knew myself. She knew I wasn't happy. She knew I was pretending. She knew who I was – she knew me when I was three.

How do I tell her? How do I apologise for all the times I hurt her, disappointed her, pushed her away, didn't hug her, withheld my love from her?

I picked up the phone and said: "Hello, this is Eileen. I just want to tell you something..."

And I told her I loved her.

I shared how I realised that I had taken my love away, it was me who silently said 'NO, I hate you'. It was me who had said I couldn't trust her; it was me who had said she betrayed me. It was me who had trapped myself in my own story. It was me who had refused to listen. It was me who had refused to speak. It was me who had rejected her and rejected myself. It was me who had been determined to be unhappy. It was me who had been drinking the poison, not realising that I would die!

No more. I'd dug deep into my own life story and I didn't like what I saw.

But there was something I could do, right then. I was an adult, not an upset child. I could re-evaluate my story and rewrite the child narrative. I could tell the truth.

Suddenly, I saw that none of what I'd made up was true. I didn't hate myself or my life. I loved my life. I had everything I needed. I had a really great life, and I thanked her profoundly for all she'd given me. I said I was sorry I made her feel guilty by blaming her for how my life had turned out. But my life had turned out exactly as I'd designed it. I got what I wanted. I got to be 'right' that she was 'wrong' to do what she did. And that had cost me everything. I was 'right' about her – it had cost me her love. I was 'right' about men – it cost me my relationships. I was right about my stammer – it cost me my self-expression. I was 'right' about myself – it cost me my self-love. I was right about my career – it cost me my satisfaction. I was right about the world – it cost me peace.

I gave up the right to be right and realised I was wrong about all of it. I looked back on my life and realised I'd punished everyone who'd loved me, including myself. I saw all my own interpretations and decisions and choices for what they were – the interpretations, decisions and choices of a scared, hurt, angry, upset child.

I was no longer that upset child. I was a grown woman. I understood and accepted my humanity. I compassionately and humbly forgave myself.

I was free to love and to trust. I was now free to be me.

A new future appeared right in front of me – empty.

What would a future of love, trust and full self-expression look like?

It looked wonderful.

It started with saying "yes". "Yes" to invitations and opportunities. Now there was no fear of being found out. I was out. I was found. I was free. I was OK. I was alive. I could breathe easily. I could speak clearly. I told the people I loved that I loved them. I fell in love with my life and the world. The world was my oyster. Anything was now possible. I was living beyond my dreams.

They say it's not about dying, but about dying with your music still inside you.

My 'music' had been rolling around in my head all my life – words, ideas, thoughts, possibilities, magic, imaginings, everything, nothing, history, time, science, space, questions, Forever – but it didn't get out of my head and into the air – not as anything clear or intelligible or intelligent, not the words I wanted, the sound or shape or sequence that made any sense, just jumbled thoughts stumbling over themselves and falling out in letters and staccato. Lost sentences.

*****

Some questions have a way of blindsiding us.

"What are you afraid of?" asked Jewel.

"Nothing," I said.

"Everyone is afraid of something," she said.

"I'm afraid of dying without ever having been known."

Wow! Where did that come from?

And how did someone like me get known?

"Write a book."

OK.

Then it hit me. Who am I to write a book? What was so important that I had to say it? Who was going to listen? Why would anyone listen to me?

I had no answers. All I ever had were questions.

But it was still there. The fear of dying having never been heard. Is this what people meant when they said 'dying with your music still inside you? An unexpressed life. Was it the real fear? Was it the fear of dying or the fear of living? Was it the fear of disappearing? Not having fully lived and then gone, as if I'd never been here? Would I be remembered? I had no children. I would be a memory for a short while. I would exist in the conversations people who knew me had about me, until either they died, or no longer remembered me, or spoke about me. I was present to a sadness, even a waste!

What was my life for?

What did I do with my life while I was here, that might live into the future?

Did it matter?

Did I matter?

I spent my life saving lives. Many people are alive and living and well because of me. But the world of the anaesthetist is not a real world. We don't figure in the reality of most people. When we meet our patients, they're asleep. They don't remember us. But they certainly place their trust, and their lives, in our hands.

How do I want to be remembered? As a writer, a thinker, a doctor, an entrepreneur, a publisher, or simply as someone who'd found the courage to shine in whatever arena she chose to show up in? Someone who loved life and played full out to the end? Someone who got a second chance to live life from "yes"?

In our own lives, we can pay a high price for not living true to ourselves, for living this one-and-only life from decisions of a small child trying to figure out how to survive and be loved and belong. It takes something to navigate this thing called Life. We land into a world already here and we have to figure out our place as we go along. When unpleasant stuff happens, and we lose some innocence, part of us dies. We don't die. We simply bury that part of ourselves – that fragile, vulnerable part – and give up on that particular aspect of ourselves that we believe is so wrong. We try to bury that bad part of ourselves, keeping it hidden and silent, essentially, we try to kill off part of ourselves, buried alive, maybe never to be set free.

What causes us to do that, to hide and pretend? Fear. Survival. What is the threat? It all seems to come down to fear of rejection and loss of love. Who will love us if we're bad and wrong? We have to hide ourselves (our love) and learn to protect ourselves from being hurt.

We learn how to protect ourselves early, thinking we're so clever and that we won't be found out, but it's a self-limiting, self-harming, self-sabotaging delusion, and we just get more practised at it as we go through life. Human beings are smart in affairs of the head, but in affairs of the heart we're all infants. We learn through the tears we cry. Some of us never learn. We go through life hoping to be discovered, but terrified of being found out. It's the words we absorb, like blotting paper, without thinking, and reinforced over time, that we then use as our own, against ourselves, that keep us trapped in our own life sentences, in a 'reality' of our own making. This is what we should fear most of all: our own power to create our own prisons. We inherit the walls, parent to child: what we should and shouldn't do, what we can and cannot do, what's good and what's evil. These age-old conversations are being repeated and recreated generation after generation, repeating our version of the past, over and over.

We need to open our eyes and ears to listen to the changing world around us, and be ready to change the world within us, by looking with new eyes and hearing with new ears.

As human beings, we complain, judge, criticise and say things that hurt. We lie and deceive and cheat and hate and betray and ... and some of us kill. And we read about that, and we make movies about that. We're fascinated by the dark side of our humanity. We don't deny it. But we also know that people are kind, that we care and support and inspire and encourage and love. So, of all the words that make us up, and all the words we use to describe the world, the words we speak, and the words we hear, we're saying them, making the choice. We choose what we say, and we choose how we listen. We're always interpreting what others are saying or doing in line with our own perceptions, or experiences, to agree or to disagree with their perspective and opinions. In truth, the only voice we actually ever listen to is our own – our own interpretation of what others say, our own expectations, our own inner voice. Yet even that voice is not our own. Someone said something once and we 'became' it. What if we started saying something different? What if we became a different kind of human being? What if we started to rewrite the story of the human race?

Words uttered by the human voice have a power like no other. On both a conscious and sub-conscious level, we abuse this power. We've all been 'hurt' by words. We've all 'hurt' with our words. We don't want to be responsible for our speaking. What if we only spoke the truth and acted on every word we spoke? What if we guarded our words with our life, if our word was sacred? What if humanity spoke in unison, with one voice? What if our words were: "there will be peace in the world"? What if our words were: "hunger will end"? What if our words were: "freedom is a human right and a collective responsibility"? What if we could trust ourselves to be true to our word?

Separate voices, speaking at once, all wanting to be heard, are simply a cacophony of noise. But think of the orchestra or the choir. Think of the power and magic of unity of purpose.

Unfortunately, even though our words are so powerful, our experience of our own voice is small and separate, wanting to be heard above a cacophony of noise. When we're speaking alone, as a small voice, it has little chance. We shout louder – desperate to be heard. We wail, then we give up, and cynically kill it off: "It doesn't work." It didn't deliver on the promise of those first miraculous utterances and the belief that we can ask for what we want and get it.

"Mama. Dada." Smiles of joy. 'Give me love.' This new voice that they are so delighted by. We try it out. But it doesn't always work so well. It lies as easily as it tells the truth. Sometimes the lie gets the reward (the love) and the truth gets the punishment (rejection).

It's confusing. This word is dangerous. This gets us into trouble. We must figure this out. Perhaps we don't want to have to be responsible for what we say. We want to forget sometimes or change our words (mind) or deny it, or even contradict it. We're confused by it, or just want to take it back. But it's already disappeared, into thin air. Where did it go? Who heard it? Did God hear it? Perhaps it landed in someone's ear, perhaps not? Perhaps they heard it or believed it, perhaps not? And perhaps it will be heard as intended and accepted, or perhaps met with an equal force to argue with it or silence it.

Ah, who was listening? Was anyone? Or is all of our conversation going on in our own head? Are we the only ones listening to what we're saying?

Mastering language is a huge task given to the small child. How do we do it? Who do we learn from? Who teaches us how to use this great power? Mostly we get to figure this out for ourselves. And often we fail. And when we fail, we turn our words on ourselves. We make ourselves the failures. We failed to be understood, to be heard, to get what we wanted, to be loved. We then become that failure, and our life becomes trying to overcome that.

This is the trap for human beings. The very 'tool' we have to liberate us, the one that allows us to create anything, becomes the thing that entraps us. We commit ourselves to our own life sentences: "I'm not wanted," "I'm not good enough," "I'm not lovable." We've discovered "no", and that's what we are now: we're "not" now.

What if that were 'not' true? What if we're all wanted, and lovable, and enough? What if there were nothing to prove? What if there was no life sentence to survive or endure?

What if there was just us, and what's happening, now, today, in the world? What if we lived like what we said mattered – really mattered. What if we really knew what was true and what wasn't true? What if we trusted those who said they loved us? What if words were the actions and the actions brought us the results we really wanted? What if we didn't have to shout to be heard? What if we used our voice only to build and create great things? What if we used our words to acknowledge, to encourage, to inspire and motivate, to empower, to express gratitude and to express love?

Without a new voice to create a new world, where will change come from? The best we can hope for is to fix and change what we judge is wrong and broken from the past. If we only speak of fighting for peace, where will true peace come from? If we only speak of overcoming fear and hate, where will trust and love and courage come from?

It must begin in our speaking. We must be willing to say something new.

We would also need to be ready to face the cynicism that already exists and the criticism that comes with ideas that challenge the comfort of the status quo. It takes courage to start to use our words in a new way, to say "yes" instead of "no", to create rather than destroy, heal rather than hurt, say words of love rather than words of hate, forgive rather than blame, liberate not dominate, empower not control, encourage not threaten, free not trap. All this is within our power.

What makes us believe we're too weak, or small or unimportant? What keeps us stuck in that story?

Is there something we can't or won't listen to? Is there some voice that we choose to listen to over another? Is there a belief we have that limits us?

I now know myself as someone who has a voice and can use that voice to empower and encourage others. My desire is to educate and inspire others to their own unlimited potential, to the power of our words, with which we are all able and capable of making a difference in the world. If I am now willing to be such a person, after so many years of selling out on my voice, what of you? What resistance would you need to give up to have your voice be heard in the world? All we need is our voice and the courage to speak. We can ask for what we want. We could also use our voice to tell the truth about ourselves and then listen to allow others to express their own truth. Miracles can happen when we listen.

Our self-expression is our responsibility, but it can only be expressed fully in an environment where we're listened to as loved, trusted and valued. Otherwise we are as 'cymbals clashing' – just making more noise, adding to the cacophony. Where you fear you're not loved and valued or believe you're not loved and valued, your self-expression withers and dies, and again you die to yourself. You are now resigned to existing as a sort of shell, the outer persona not true to your inner being. You occur to yourself as a fraud. Who you present to the world, who people think you are, this isn't who you are. This is the persona you created to allow you to fit in, to belong, not trusting that your own self was good enough. This is the good news. You are good enough. You're still here, waiting to be liberated, by the truth. The truth will set you free. You are lovable and loved. You deserve your own love, compassion and forgiveness. Give yourself the courage to shine. You don't need permission.

CHAPTER 7

The Truth Sometimes Hurts

*"If you tell the truth you don't have to remember anything" – **Mark Twain***

I retired from the Health Service in 2014 – after thirty-two years. There were several 'pointers' to this decision. It was offered to me as a possible choice in an "early retirement package" even though I considered myself too young to retire. It was do-able with some 'downsizing' of my lifestyle. However, the deciding factor for me was a moral imperative when the refurbished theatres proudly declared that the new operating tables could now hold patients weighing 450 kg.

This occurred to me as a serious failure of my profession. This was evidence that we as doctors – in leading health care – had failed. The numbers don't lie – they tell their own story. I felt I could no longer participate (collude) in a system that said it was OK for a human being to weigh 450 kg.

Was political correctness more important than health? Was the conversation for obesity to be avoided at all costs for fear of upsetting people? It was obvious people were already upset. What was more important than people's health? Were children to be permitted to damage their health simply because responsible adults didn't want to offend their young offspring – to not upset them by telling them the truth – maybe they are overweight? And maybe there is something else they are trying to communicate. It's as if we're all blind! The numbers don't lie – they tell their own story. What about the other excesses? It's not just food we turn to for comfort. Is it just that adults don't want to be responsible for their own actions either?

We're now swimming in a culture of pretence and dishonesty in fear that our livelihoods, friendships or relationships will be damaged if we tell the truth. Is the truth being sacrificed in the interest of being accepted, liked, popular, 'nice', even being voted back into power? This silent agreement that it's OK to be as unhealthy as we want now is completely ignoring the fact that the impact will have to be dealt with later, if not sooner. There's a personal cost to the life of the individual. There's an impact on friends and family, and society itself will have to pick up the tab! There'll be no escape – the human body doesn't work outside a healthy weight. As it is, the health care system is overburdened by the inevitable consequences of lifestyle diseases such as stress and diabetes. The psychological impact of obesity on young people is huge – identity, bullying, depression and suicide. So much self-inflicted injury by people not being aware of the consequences of their choices.

We cannot underestimate the psychological impact and damage of overconsumption or addictive behaviour. This is huge, no matter how 'acceptable' we make the package. At least we can see 450 kg on a human body. We cannot see the equivalent weight on the human mind, where the emotional pain and suffering is likely to be of equal magnitude. Young people have to navigate the turbulent waters of identity and belonging and feelings of unworthiness and failure, in a culture of bullying and shame. Ignoring what is underlying weight gain, body image, poor self-esteem and self-harm is just adding to the psychological impact, the likely consequences of which will manifest in the future. As doctors, we need to speak openly and honestly about what challenges each of us as human beings, doing our best to deal with the ups and downs of life, and encourage coping mechanisms that don't damage the quality of our lives.

Patients turn to doctors as a first port of call in their distress. Doctors must be available to listen. And, then who do doctors turn to? We must be willing to share our own humanity in this regard. Doctors are human too. First, "Do No Harm", but equally: "Physician, heal thyself"! A doctor not willing to address their own responsibility as a healthy role model, will not be trusted by their patients to do what's necessary. We are each judged by our actions, not our words. For each of us, doctor and patient, we need our anchors: a strong internal compass, trusted companions and empowering language that consistently build our resources and resilience, protecting us from the dangers of negative thinking, depression, self-harm, despair and suicide.

Words are of no value if we can't hear them, if we're not listening to them. And we don't listen because we think people lie, or we just don't want to know! But listen we must. And then trust ourselves to know when we hear the truth. We must have the courage to engage, listen, to hear what's being said. We may not like it, but until we hear it, we cannot deal with what is being said.

Most of all, we must discover whose commentary we're listening to when another is speaking. Are our own inner thoughts drowning out the other's words? Are we already programmed to hear what we think we want to hear? Are we turning a deaf ear to what we truly need to listen to? Listening requires courage. Listening might require that we change our opinion or our point of view. Listening can be uncomfortable.

As adults, we value our right to choose and our freedom of choice. Sometimes we forget that with rights come responsibilities. We can choose freely, but we're not necessarily free from the consequences of our choices. This becomes very apparent when we're faced with the effects of things like smoking, overconsumption of alcohol, drug-taking, excessive calorie consumption, and risky or illegal behaviour like drink-driving. The consequences of these behaviours can be devastating to our health, and to the health of others, and to our wealth, both personally and as a society as we pay the cost. Applying legal or financial sanctions and a threat of punishment are not only a poor substitute for education and empowering people to engage in responsible behaviour, they're obviously less effective and certainly cost us dearly.

What I observed in the Pre-Anaesthesia Assessment Clinic, when meeting people coming for surgical procedures who were at higher risk of peri-operative complications because of certain conditions, was that encouraging people to be responsible for their own health and well-being is challenging. We're so conditioned to blame outside circumstances for our own condition: "I can't help it," "it's my genes," "my job is too stressful," "I'm depressed," "it's in the family," etc. However, we're the drivers of our own lives. We make all our own choices: who we listen to, who we ignore, whose advice we take, what excuses or reasons we want to use. When someone suggests we're not being responsible, we react thinking we're being blamed. We seem to forget that we are already responsible for our own life, and if it's not going well, then maybe we have something to do with that. The fact is, as adults, we feel we have the right to do whatever we want to do, whenever we want to do it, and we don't want anyone else telling us what we should and should not do.

And that goes for our relationship with doctors. We all know 'prevention is better than cure'. That does not stop the vast numbers of patients ignoring the advice of their doctors about the dangers of unhealthy lifestyle choices. There are also many doctors who don't follow their own advice, so why should patients listen? Is there something that doctors themselves aren't listening to? What is being communicated in the unsaid?

The problem is, in our abundant, 'developed' world, where we have so much of everything at our fingertips, we're being marketed to every moment of every day. What stops us from consumption overload, other than our own willpower? Without extraordinary willpower, it seems like we've no defence against the vast consumer industry enticing us to buy more – more fast food, more information, stronger alcohol, better entertainment, more TV channels. Everything is coming at us so fast, we don't have time to think and evaluate – "Do I need this?" "Is this nourishing for me?" "Can I afford it?"

And what about the younger people? In Celtic Tiger Ireland, no one said "no". Just "What do you want?". "What flavour?". "The blue one or the red one?"

In a world of endless choices, how do people know what they want?

We generally want what we see, so it seems like we want all of it, now. We're all children in the sweet shop. And when we can't have it all now, when our relationships, or our career, or our finances don't instantly work out, what do we do? We reach for the instant gratification – something to numb the reality, to avoid the pain. Drink? Drugs? Lie down? Get depressed? Commit suicide?

We need to ask ourselves what works and what doesn't work, for our bodies and our minds, for our relationships, our finances, our spiritual and emotional well-being, for our lives, and to stop doing what clearly doesn't work. We need to listen to something other than our own thoughts. We need to trust those who say they love us. We need to be that someone for ourselves, whom we love and trust. We have everything we need to be our own best friend. We can then befriend another. Alone we can do so little. We get through together.

It all starts with awareness. Are we aware of what are we saying, and what are we listening to? Is our own communication open, clear, honest, straight? This is the challenge. This is what takes courage. This is risking speaking our truth and being willing to stand by what we say. It takes listening to another such that we can know them by what they say. This isn't what we normally do. We speak to be accepted. We listen to agree. We speak to be liked. We listen for our turn. We speak to fit in. We listen to be right. We speak to look good in front of others. We listen to differentiate. We speak to get away with things. We pretend that we're listening. We lie. It can't be just me! It must be a human trait. It's how we learn to deal with this 'facility' we call language. We learnt it as children and got to practise some really bad habits. Perhaps we need a new set of language skills as adults. We need to get past our young sibling-sibling or adult-child conversations.

We need to be free to move on into full adulthood, responsible for what goes into and comes out of our mouths. The world is at stake. If the trajectory of our entire life can be based on the (mis)interpretation and a (mis)understanding of a child, and we spend most our lives trying to fix and change where we 'went wrong' as children, what could be possible if we truly behaved as fully responsible adults?

What if there wasn't anything wrong with any of us?

What if 'wrong' were simply a child's interpretation, but the only word available in our young vocabulary, to explain what happened to us/them? Something inexplicable happened, and we trapped it in language.

Perhaps nothing is wrong. Perhaps we're not wrong. Perhaps we were never broken. Perhaps we're perfect just the way we are, and we always were.

I just spoke the way I spoke. It didn't mean I was wrong and ugly and stupid and useless, and would have to spend my life proving that, and in failing to do so, simply make the entire world wrong anyway so I fit right in! Perhaps I could've spared myself the trouble and simply spoke the way I spoke, feeling the fear and doing it anyway.

But now, look at all the pent-up words I have, tumbling out in this book. It was all perfect anyway!

Even if I don't get to spare you any anguish, consider your life is unfolding exactly as it's supposed to, and you're in the perfect place.

Maybe there are some of you who also got trapped in your version of this suffer-punish cycle. 'I'll use my life suffering to punish you for what you did!' The more we suffer, the worse they should feel, and the more we punish them, so they will suffer. 'So the more I screw up my life, the more I hope you will feel bad about it.' Who's actually suffering? Who are we really punishing? Who do we want to suffer more than ourselves? Who has hurt us unforgivably? My poor mother. What she had to endure from her ungrateful daughter. Maybe that is the lot of mothers. They do their best, with what they have, what they perhaps got from their own mothers, and it's not enough for us. We want more. They didn't give us what we wanted, or enough of what we wanted – love, attention – when we wanted it. They said they loved us. We said: "That's a lie. If you loved me, you would do x, or you wouldn't do y." They did what they did. We said: "They loved something/someone more than me." And we punish them for that. And we wreck our lives to prove how much "they shouldn't have done what they did".

Perhaps when I found 'success' in the world of anaesthesia, I really believed I was winning on all counts. I was in a profession I respected with colleagues I admired. It was a speciality I enjoyed and was skilled at. I had all the trappings of success. – status, money, authority. I was admired and respected by my peers and my patients.

Was that enough? For a while, yes. It allowed me to contribute. It allowed me to make a difference. But was it the fullest expression of my potential to contribute, to make the difference I wanted to make?

Ultimately, no, because it also allowed me to hide. There was no demand for me to be heard.

Did I fall asleep, anaesthetised from my own upset, my own unfulfilled expectations, failed relationships, thwarted intentions, my 'real' self, alienated from my authentic voice, my authentic self-expression?

Hidden and silent in the rarefied and privileged world of anaesthesia wasn't the same as being willing to risk being seen and heard in a wider world where telling the truth is scary, and not everyone wants to hear what you have to say.

One of the huge fears people would express before surgery is: "What if I say something while I'm asleep? Can people speak when they're anaesthetised?"

Some people don't drink alcohol for fear their disinhibition might 'let the cat out of the bag', that their 'secret' might get out. There isn't much freedom in this guarded life.

As Mam often said: "We're only as sick as our secrets."

CHAPTER 8

The Joy of Speaking

"Life is a daring adventure, or nothing" – **Helen Keller**

"Hello."

I had not set foot in a classroom since I was their age. A school classroom. And there I was, preparing to deliver a 'speech'!!

The memories came flooding back – of the anxiety, apprehension, terror, the dry mouth. It was thirty years since I'd vowed never to speak in public, and six months after my epiphany moment at the microphone. In that extraordinary six months, I accomplished things I never believed I would, including the reason I was standing there, ready, willing and able to tell the tale about it – my trip to the 'Roof of Africa', climbing Mount Kilimanjaro.

Breathe.

I looked at the class of forty teenagers aged sixteen to seventeen in front of me and took a deep breath. Then I looked again. And I saw – young people – each of them looking at me, waiting. I could almost hear them: "Who is she? What is she going to say now? What IS she wearing? How old is she? How long will this last?"

They looked bored. Or did they? Were they just waiting? For me to prove myself? To show them that I deserved their time and attention? So I started...

"Hello. Thank you for inviting me here. My name is Eileen Forrestal. I was born and raised in Dublin, Ireland. I now live in the north-west of Ireland –Sligo – 'Yeats Country'. I can see Ben Bulben's head from my garden.

(What follows is a slightly longer version of what I shared that day in the classroom. I am taking the liberty of using this opportunity to introduce myself to you as I knew myself in the world back then.)

"I'm a medical doctor. I've worked as an anaesthetist for many years, mostly in Ireland but also in the UK, Canada and Africa. I love my work, not only because it gives me an opportunity to travel, but it gives me an opportunity to contribute to people and make a difference in their lives. It has given me great success and a great life, and it was a very good career choice.

"I was just seventeen when I went to medical school. I qualified in 1982. The country was in recession and I left almost immediately to work in England. I've worked in many different countries and different areas of medicine since then. I trained initially as a general practitioner and I worked and travelled a lot overseas in developing countries. I learnt a lot about people. In many countries, it's a daily struggle for survival. There's huge inequality in the areas of health and education. In countries at war, the desperate search for food and water by the hungry is overshadowed by the forces that struggle for the lofty ideals of identity, peace, justice, freedom and self-determination.

"As a medical student, I spent three months working in a small hospital in a South African homeland: Bophuthatswana. This was the time of severe apartheid and the brutal Idi Amin regime in neighbouring Uganda. I didn't feel good or proud to be a white person. It made no difference what I thought or believed, or said, how compassionate or humbled I felt, how embarrassed or guilty I felt, because of my white colour, an accident of birth. I was seen as white, privileged – I was treated as white, and I was feared and hated as white. The babies screamed in terror as we approached to vaccinate or weigh or measure their tiny bodies. The older children stared. And with the Afrikaners, I was despised as a 'kaffir lover'. Trapped again, in a white, healthy, privileged body, and in other people's opinions of me.

"No escape.

"In my travels throughout the developing world, I witnessed a lot of poverty and the struggle for survival of so many people. This led me to be involved in many fundraising projects over the years, especially those delivering health and education opportunities in the poorer African countries, Nepal and Cambodia.

"These charitable endeavours have have contributed much to my extraordinary life. While I raised money for these worthy causes, money that wouldn't have been raised had I not chosen to do that, I've had unique opportunities to experience aspects of life that I'd never have experienced otherwise, and for this I'm forever grateful.

"Thank you for being part of my fundraising drive to raise the money for Mukuru slum and school in Nairobi. This gave me the opportunity to do something amazing: not just raising money and awareness but also raising my own level of courage.

"I've rafted the Zambezi. I've flown a microlite over Victoria Falls. I've been on The Road to Mandalay. I've bathed in the Ganges; ridden an elephant in Thailand and ostrich in South Africa; hypnotised a chicken in the Philippines; boated across Lake Titicaca; trekked to Everest Base Camp; but my experience of this trip to Kilimanjaro offered me something unique, a discovery that will last my lifetime.

"However, the reason I went ... wasn't to do something adventurous in my life – I was used to doing that. This particular trip was different. This trip only came about as a matter of my word, not out of a desire to do something I'd always wanted to do. It was a conversation at a microphone six months ago that had me realise I could create my own life with my own words.

"I was challenged to be someone who could be relied on to honour their word and keep their promise. I didn't always know myself to be such a person.

"I mostly knew myself as someone who wouldn't give my word to anything so I couldn't break it, or give my word to doing quite simple things that would be easy for me to honour, or, what had been my particular flavour, give my word and almost immediately be looking for a way out that would be entirely reasonable as to why I couldn't do what I said I'd do.

"What I was now being asked to do was give my word to something I had no idea about or how to do it, and go and do it anyway, to say yes first and figure it out later.

"In the hospital where I worked, there was an older man who regularly took groups of people on a trip to Kilimanjaro and Nairobi, raising funds for a slum school. I'd never spoken to him but admired what he did from afar as he got regular mentions in the local newspaper. I saw him by chance in a supermarket and decided to use the opportunity to say hello and congratulate him on his good work over the years. Almost immediately he asked: 'Would you like to come on our next trip?' I could feel the familiar excuses coming to my tongue: 'Ah, no, I don't have the time,' 'I'm not fit,' 'I'm no good at climbing'... And stopped.

"What if I just said 'yes'? What if I said 'yes' without knowing what was involved, and actually went? Wow. What would that be like! I'd no idea. I wasn't yet practised in saying a 'yes' I could reliably trust myself to deliver on, so I said: 'OK.'

"He said: 'We're going in March.' I said: 'OK.' He said: 'You need to raise €3500.' I said 'OK,' and that was it. The rest is history.

"What I didn't say was: How am I going to raise the money? How am I going to get the time off? How am I going to be able to climb Mount Kilimanjaro? What am I doing going to Tanzania? They were the questions that came after the 'yes'. Discovering the answers was the interesting part. I was taught one of the greatest lessons of my life on that trip.

"The trek up Mount Kilimanjaro takes four days. We started off, full of joviality and enthusiasm, with just a tiny touch of trepidation, at the gates of Kilimanjaro National Park. There was a group of us, twenty in all, including our guides. We were climbing with an organisation called Childaid, which had been formed by members of the Irish Army who had served in Rwanda and had seen the suffering and horrors of war and its impact on children, and were now giving back, so we also had soldiers in our group, to protect us.

"I loved the occasion of it: the experience, the newness, the excitement, the adventure, the not knowing. I now considered myself fearless in these situations: meeting new people, chatting contentedly one on one – relaxed, walk, talk, think, breathe, rest, enjoy. And my usual – I'd go as far as I could and then I'd stop, turn around and go back. No pressure.

"That was my plan. I'd no ambition to get to the top, or even to complete the climb beyond what I knew I could safely do. I had raised the money. I would do my best. I wouldn't risk my health or push myself beyond my limits. I was clear. I would do what I could do, and no more.

"So, we carried on. Poli, Poli. Slowly, slowly. And 'if you think you are going slowly, go even slower' was the instruction from our guides, seasoned trekkers at altitude. Music to my ears. I was in no rush. The land was beautiful. The weather was perfect. The company was great. I was happy. We climbed higher.

"As a medic, I was aware of the condition of altitude sickness, which was a serious possibility when trekking at altitude. There could be life-threatening complications of pulmonary oedema – the lungs filling up with fluid to cause an 'internal drowning'. or cerebral oedema, where the brain swells in its enclosed skull casing causing unconsciousness, stroke or death.

"So, definitely, I was on the lookout for signs and symptoms in myself and in my fellow trekkers and would beat a hasty retreat or sound an alarm at the earliest indication. As a precaution, I'd brought some Acetazolamide tablets, which might have limited benefit in an emergency. As it happened, when I arrived at the last camp before the final ascent, at around 5 p.m. in the evening, I got a splitting headache and it seemed like my brain was trying to escape out through my eyeballs. I considered this an emergency, that I was possibly in danger of an imminent stroke, and took two tablets, tried to swallow some noodle soup, and went straight to bed. We were due to resume climbing at midnight – I wasn't too optimistic about that!

"Bed was the top bunk at the very back of the dormitory. There were many already sleeping in the occupied bunks. My boots made an embarrassingly loud noise as I crossed the wooden floor. 'SSSHHHHHSSSHHH!!!!'

"I climbed to my allocated bunk and began to unpeel the layers. It was freezing. My fingers could just about untie the laces of my boots, which I left at the bottom of the bed. I took off my balaclava, my neck cowl, my hat, my jacket, my jumper, down to my underlayers and then added another layer of sleep gear and struggled into the sleeping bag. I fumbled to pull the hood and the tie around my face so only my nose was visible. I was exhausted.

"Immediately, I got an urge to pee. The realisation that the two tablets were diuretics hit me, and I wouldn't be able to hold it till the morning. There wasn't anything for it but to get up and go to the loo. I peeled myself out of the sleeping bag, put on my layers of jumpers and jackets and balaclava and hat and gloves, and crept down the ladder with my shoes. The floor was FREEZING. I put on my boots best I could. I crept across the wooden floor. 'SSHHSSSSHHHH!' came the

131

impatient, disembodied voices from the darkness. My little torch lit a way through the bunks. Out the door, pitch dark, snowing, a freezing blizzard when I turned the corner and headed for the solitary lit hut across the yard. As I approached the hut; the stench made me want to throw up. So, quickly deciding to pee outside, I went beyond the light into the darkness – no moon, no stars, pitch black – and peeled the layers again to pee on the side of the mountain, on the edge of the abyss. But ahhh, what relief!

"And back to the hut, to the bunk, to the peeling off of the outer layers, to the re-clothing with new layers, to shuffling back down into the sleeping bag, tightening the string around my face so only the tip of my nose could feel the freezing air, to breathe. To sleep...

"But no. Not again! The same sensation: the urge to pee. Please, please, no. NO... NO... It was no use. I couldn't risk wetting myself and the sleeping bag and the bunk. There wasn't anything to do but go through the whole process again.

"And again.

"And again.

"And again.

"Five times that night I peed on the black edge of a frozen world.

"At midnight we were called to get up.

"Time to go, to make the ascent to catch the sunrise.

"No way, I whimpered. Not yet, please. Just five more minutes. I was just drifting off. But already the urge to pee again.

"It was hopeless. I got up, dressed, peed and, before long, I was sitting silently with other tired faces, eating gloopy porridge for breakfast, trying to swallow, reassuring myself I'd start but I'll be turning back from here. 'I'm exhausted. I've done enough. This is as far as I'm going to get.'

"I went outside to find my group and explain my decision. It was still snowing through the pitch blackness, the snowflakes being illuminated by our headlights. I could hear murmuring around me. I recognised the voices of my team, and shuffled over: "I don't think I'll be going too far today folks" Best of luck. See you at the bottom.'

"It was after midnight. The plan was to be at the top for 6 a.m., to get the sunrise. My plan was how to get off this insufferable mountain as quickly as possible before I died of the cold or something else.

"'Hello. I'm Douglas, your guide.'

"'Hi Douglas, I'm Eileen. I don't think I'll get too far.'

"'Let's go,' said Douglas. 'This way.'

"'Where? I can't see any path or lights.'

"'Up,' he said.

"I looked up. Like up a wall. There were tiny lights snaking up an almost perpendicular against the blackness. 'You must be joking?!'

I heard someone retching and vomiting to my left. 'Are you OK?' 'Yeah. Fine.' Good. Disembodied voices.

"I started. One foot in front of the other. One step at a time. Lifting, climbing. After ten steps I was exhausted: 'Douglas. I'm sorry. I'm very tired. I had no sleep.'

"'It's OK. You are good. You are strong. One more step. This way.'

"I took three more steps. And stopped.

"'Don't stop. Just one more step. This way.' I took two more steps.

"'I can't do this, Douglas. I'm freezing. I can't feel my feet. I can't feel my hands. I'm tired. I just want to sleep.'

"'No, don't sleep. One more step.'

"'I'll die on this mountain. You must take me down. Please let me sleep.'

"'One more step. You are strong. You are good. Don't sleep.'

"I had no energy to argue. I looked below. There were lights below. People were behind me, slower than me, snaking up.

"One more step.

"We continued. 'One more step. Don't sleep. You are strong.' I no longer resisted. I did as I was told. 'One more step. Don't sleep.'

Douglas walked with me for ten hours.

"The darkness was fading; light was beginning. I was no longer my body. I was frozen beyond cold, beyond suffering, just listening to Douglas' words of encouragement, now starting to believe him.

"We met the rest of the group coming down. 'It's fantastic. Keep going. You're nearly there. Take your time. Just get there.'

"We emerged above the clouds. The sun came up over the Serengeti. It shone on a magical universe. I was here, on top of the world, not giving up. I saw someone was behind me, about 500 metres down. I could hear his guide encouraging him, as Douglas did me. There was just the two of us on the mountain now, with our guides. He was looking up to me. I had to get there for his sake. I couldn't abandon him now.

"We got to the summit.

"I was astounded. I was beyond cold, but so delighted with my accomplishment, full of love and gratitude for Douglas. He got me there. He didn't sell out on me. He didn't give up on me. I was willing to give up on myself, to sell out on myself. I wanted to believe what I thought I 'knew' about myself, that 'I couldn't do it.' I had wanted to give up so many times, but he stood his ground for me.

"To be that strong for another human being, to stand for their achievement, for what they can accomplish, to trust yourself to know them better than they know themselves, to not be afraid to walk beside them and pick them up if they fall. This is true courage: to encourage another in the face of their resignation, their defeat, to keep them going, to get them where you know they can, and want to go, to be their guide to the mountaintop."

They listened. They listened while I shared the entire experience, including the visit to the slum school where we handed over the money we had raised so the children there could have copies and pencils and a hot meal. They really listened. They were fascinated. They asked questions. They looked at the photographs. They saw something. They realised that education was a privilege in this world, and they were some of the lucky ones. They realised that they took so much for granted. There was a seventeen-year-old in our climbing group, and they realised it was entirely possible for a brave teenager to make a difference in the world.

They listened to me.

I saw that what I said made a difference for them.

It provided a window into a wider world where they too could choose to play. Me being here in front of them, speaking, was a miracle for me – and the fact they were listening was a dream come true.

And I said that too. And they got it.

Life was scary outside your comfort zone, but it could be amazing. It wasn't easy, but it was definitely worth it.

Since then, I've trekked to Everest Base Camp, parachuted from an airplane, and cycled from Ho Chi Minh City to Angkor Wat.

I would never have done these things 'for myself'. But in doing them, I witnessed so much more. I've been angered by the injustice and inequality I've witnessed, shocked at the poverty and deprivation, embarrassed by the smug satiety of the West, horrified at the thoughtless destruction of 'progress' and saddened by the ignorance, lack of empathy and compassion for the suffering of our fellow human beings.

I had the surreal experience of raffling six water filters between 88 impoverished families in a land-mined region at the Cambodian-Thai border and, days later, I was enjoying a spectacular firework display in Disneyland, California!!

But this is the way the world is. I'm the lucky one with the passport, the freedom to travel, to speak, to vote. I'm one with a voice. It's up to me to use the voice I've been gifted with to speak for those who have no voice, no opportunity to be heard, no freedom to speak. The reality is, we all have a voice. Not everyone has the privilege of being listened to. Have we the courage to say what needs to be said, to encourage, to empower, to liberate? Have we the courage to listen to what we don't want to hear? That is the question I ask myself, every day. What am I afraid of? In the words of Eleanor Roosevelt: "You must do the thing you think you cannot do."

I'm determined that all people know themselves to be powerful and able and capable of making a difference in the world, no matter what their circumstances. We all have the resources we need. And for those we don't have, we can ask for. We all have a voice. We need to use it to tell the truth about how the world is for us, and what we want to do about that.

I'm conscious how deafness can cause us to disconnect from what we can't, or don't, want to hear, and that without taking a stand and raising our voice, how limited our contribution is. It takes courage to stand up and speak. It also takes courage to sit down and listen.

CHAPTER 9

Finding my Place

"Your playing small does not serve the world".
– Marianne Williamson

From Bedside to Bali and Beyond

I first got involved with my beloved 'diary' in 2006. I had bought it every year since 2001 and used it as my daily survivor's diary – anaesthesia was a very stressful speciality – being the sole anaesthetist on call at night or on weekends for 250,000 people was a lonely and anxiety-provoking experience. The simple words of wisdom in my little diary helped me survive those early years after the breakdown of my marriage and my return home to Ireland.

In 2006, I decided to participate in a fundraising cycle challenge through Vietnam and Cambodia for ActionAid. Not being particularly imaginative about fundraising, I looked to my diary for inspiration. Not reading anything particularly helpful, I considered the possibility that perhaps the person who produced the diary – obviously a very thoughtful person – might be persuaded to give me some of the proceeds from her Christmas sales for my fundraising! The shop that supplied my diary directed me to Strandhill, only five miles away, where Glenda lived. I knocked on her door.

She invited me in and we had a lovely conversation which culminated, however, in her telling me she was no longer doing the diaries. Her husband, the inspiration for them, had recently died, and while she got great solace and power from the diaries that helped her deal with his prolonged illness, with this new and unexpected turn in her life, she was no longer interested in carrying on with them alone.

Then, unexpectedly, she asked if I might be interested in a business partnership. Again, with some hesitation but willing, I said "yes". Anything to save my beloved diary.

I had some money I was willing to invest, and within a few weeks we had a new name, a new business plan, and a new colourful edition – *The Irish Get Up and Go Diary 2007* was ready for sale.

Neither Glenda nor I were experienced in sales, so my partner at the time, seeing there was an obvious downturn coming in the construction sector, decided to jump ship, believing he could easily turn his hand from bricks to books. He turned out to be a natural salesman and happily travelled the country offering retailers "an irresistible offer" if they would stock the diaries. Sales steadily grew and we applied to appear on *Dragons' Den* in 2010. I thought if we could attract the attention of Norah Casey, we would be on our way. Unfortunately, we didn't have a digital strategy at the time, so we didn't secure her investment, but the learning was invaluable, and we ended up happy to be one of the ones that got away.

We continued like this for the next couple of years, with Glenda and I creating the diaries in our spare time, keeping up with our 'day jobs' while our sales man 'extraordinaire' hit the road.

Life sometimes throws curveballs, but it also throws us a lifeline to the future we could so easily miss. In late September 2013, I received a phone call out of the blue, from a woman in The Czech Republic, Bea, whom I'd known somewhat briefly years earlier. Bea was inviting me to attend a Women Only Entrepreneur Retreat at a private, purpose-built resort in Bali, for a month, in November. My initial reaction was: "No, I'm not an entrepreneur; I'm an anaesthetist." I couldn't possibly take a month off, and anyway it was too expensive, and too short notice. She said 'fine' and hung up.

Realising that my company was called Get Up and Go and I rarely said no these days, almost immediately I phoned her back, willing to be persuaded, and asked her to tell me a bit more about it. Why had she thought of me, and what I could expect to get out of it?

"Oh. I just thought that with your *Get Up and Go Diaries*, you might be interested in growing your market globally to impact more people."

Well, wow! Having put it that way, yes, I was definitely interested.

After a short discussion, I said: "Yes, I'll go." It sounded like a really exciting opportunity, and it was simply a matter of negotiating the time off. The operating theatres were being refurbished, so the workload was reduced, and unpaid leave was an option.

She then said I'd need to do a profile test. Prior to this interaction with Bea, I knew nothing of the creative genius of Roger James Hamilton, and his unique profiling system. To get maximum value from attending the entrepreneur retreat, I was encouraged to take the test and discover: "What kind of entrepreneur are you?" At that time, I definitely didn't consider myself an entrepreneur. I was an anaesthetist – happily working in my local hospital. However, with my fledgling business, the invitation to consider the possibility of growing this business to a level where we could impact globally was a compelling reason to jump in and participate in the month-long programme. So, out of curiosity, I said: "Sure, what harm can it do?" It was a fifteen-minute online test – no big deal.

I took the test the following day. My result said I was a Star Profile[2] with 48 per cent "Dynamo Energy", 38 per cent "Blaze Energy", 4 per cent "Steel Energy" and 10 per cent "Tempo Energy". I could just about grasp the idea of the energy, but a Star Profile?! Me? In my line of work, I wear a mask; no one knows who I am. Was I a Star hiding out in the silent world of anaesthesia??

A month later, I was in an entrepreneur intensive retreat in the beautiful paradise island of Bali.

I'd first visited Bali in 1984 on an independent travel adventure following the hippie trail – the Bangkok to Bali Rover – with my *Lonely Planet Guide to Southeast Asia*. I'd been working as a junior anaesthetist in Worthing in Sussex with a registrar called Mike. After a quiet bank holiday weekend where I'd stayed home, watching TV and munching my way through several packets of Tayto crisps, Maltesers, and treating myself to a few glasses of cheap red wine – I would rarely

2 One of the eight profiles in Roger James Hamilton's Wealth / Talent Dynamics Profiling System. Wealth Dynamics is the world's leading profiling tool for entrepreneurs, used by over 1 million entrepreneurs worldwide to find their 'flow'. Discovering your profile can unlock your natural path to wealth, flow and fulfilment. https://wealthdynamics.geniusu.com

drink alone but was feeling particularly sorry for myself – I gladly returned to work, and people, on the Tuesday.

"How was your weekend?"

"Quiet. Yours?"

"Excellent. Got some great photos of a total eclipse of the sun on Bali. I'll show you when I get the negatives developed."

What? Bali? For the weekend? Do people do that sort of thing? Apparently, some do. My mind was blown. We spoke about Bali and travel and going beyond the expected 'normal' and what was available beyond our comfort zone, stepping into the unknown. He showed me photos of his travels in Colombia, and Brazil, and Zanzibar. Crikey!

I was hooked. I couldn't wait to get to a travel agent to see what was out there. I never had this kind of conversation in Dublin. Heathrow was up the road and my gateway to the world. I discovered Trailfinders. Their brochures were magical. Places I'd only read about came alive. They were actual destinations. They existed. I just needed a passport, vaccinations and time off. All could be arranged.

I left Heathrow Airport with a one-way ticket to Bangkok and six weeks of freedom ahead. I was exhilarated and terrified. What if I died, kidnapped, raped, poisoned, lost? I was willing to risk it. I wanted photos like Mike. I wanted to explore the world. I wanted to know what was out there. I had one life and I was determined to live it, now. What if I died young and never got the chance? I was off on my adventures – me and my trust in God.

Bali was my last stop – I'd travelled from Bangkok, to Phuket, to Ko Samui, to Penang, to Singapore, to Java, and arrived in paradise. My experience was of coming home. I couldn't explain it. Heaven on earth. I stayed three weeks, in beach huts, exploring by motorbike, sunrises, sunsets, temples, paddy fields, flowers. The freedom, the peace, the beauty of the landscape, the people and the traditions were exquisite. It was like I belonged there. My heart knew where it was. I could die happy here.

And there I was, thirty years later, feeling like I'd just come home.

One thing was certain, I was going to make the most of it while I was there. Vison Villas was fabulous! And I was excited to meet Roger, the creator of the Wealth Dynamic Profile System and this amazing entrepreneur retreat.

Roger appeared for his first session on Thursday afternoon. He is a tall, handsome man, with an accent and appearance that makes it difficult to locate him (his mother is Chinese, his father Scottish, and he was educated in architecture in Cambridge, England). We introduced ourselves. I explained I was a doctor from Ireland with a small business producing inspirational, motivational diaries. He asked me what Profile I was, and I answered, somewhat sheepishly: "Star profile."

He responded: "Oh, you don't find too many Stars in medicine. Do you specialise?"

"Yes, anaesthesia."

"Wow. What is it like for a Star to be an anaesthetist?"

I hesitated, then answered: "Honestly, I think it exhausting!"

As I looked back through my career, I saw how constrained I'd been, trying to conform to how I thought a doctor should be, like it didn't come naturally. I was definitely happiest when I could 'shine a light' on something, or someone: explaining, recommending a good book or film, or restaurants or a country to visit, always pointing out things that perhaps others hadn't seen, always trying educate or enlighten or encourage people to explore or discover new things for themselves, to be who they wanted to be.

But there I was, in a career that had me putting people to sleep, putting tubes down their throats, drugging them into unconsciousness, stifling their self-expression, putting them in the dark, turning off the light. The dichotomy was startling. I was definitely considering the possibility I was in the wrong job.

Anyway, Roger was the mentor and this was my opportunity to discover something new: to practise the natural strengths and talents of the Star profile for a month while I was here, to see how that fitted with my personality and what I wanted to achieve with my business and how best to develop and use my skills to grow it in the future.

I spent the month as a 'Star' and loved it. It was so easy just to 'shine a light' on what I was doing: on the diaries, on what I wanted to achieve, on my vision for the future, getting clearer on my passion and my purpose. I was a natural promoter. I discovered social media and graphic design and promotion plans and logo design and branding and Google analytics and video and storytelling. There were also budgets and revenue and cash flow and profit, mindset and collaboration, value and leverage, and so much more. I taught Jewel how to swim. And I started to write this book...

I returned home after the month, and back to work in my hospital. Now what?

I'd tasted life as an entrepreneur and could see what was possible.

But I was still a doctor and there was work to be done. I'd decide later.

My first list back was gynaecology in the newly refurbished obstetric theatre, where the numbers were there, in black on the new whiteboard on the wall outside the theatre...

"450 kg".

That was it!

At that moment, I knew I was out.

I realised I didn't want to continue to put people to sleep. There had to be another way for me to make a difference in people's lives. I wanted people to be inspired by who they were, to live happy and healthy lives – the great lives they wanted for themselves. My Star profile and 'dynamo energy' could be put to better use, and it was now time to wake people up!

With my new vision for my life, I saw I was more interested in empowering people to be at the source of their own health and well-being than being part of an overburdened, paternalistic system, trying to fix what need not get broken in the first place. I didn't want to follow the disease any more. I wanted to nip it in the bud. I wanted to interrupt the predictable narrative. I wanted to be part of the movement leading a new conversation for health – by getting to the source of the 'dis-ease'.

I felt I'd been sleepwalking for years and had just woken up!

*****

When I finally retired, one year later in 2014, I was ready to focus all my efforts on getting these diaries out into the wider world for greater impact. We knew by then these simple books were making a positive difference in people's lives.

The Star profile gave me freedom to shine outside the limitations of the medical profession. The Entrepreneur Movement gave me a place to meet and connect with more purpose-inspired social entrepreneurs, to tap into, and contribute to, the bigger conversations. It shone a light onto a new and exciting path, opening up new opportunities and revealing more arenas where I could fully express myself. I loved being at play in this new world of possibility.

I now felt free and empowered to shine a light for others to follow and delight in their discovery that they, too, could shine in their own life and be a light for others. My passion was, and is, to inspire and encourage people to live happy, healthy and fulfilled lives, free to be themselves, shining in the art of living.

As a doctor, using my one pair of hands, I was limited in how much impact I could have in the world, how much encouragement I could share. I believed that in sharing the wise words quoted in the diaries, I would have an impact on many more people than I could ever reach as a doctor.

I could now push on at full speed with my new venture – as an entrepreneur – going beyond life as I'd known it.

I'd spent more than thirty years dealing with 'sick people'. I was well aware of the consequences of ill health – physical, emotional or mental. It robbed people of vitality, aliveness, choice and opportunity. On the one hand, I observed people who were terribly ill physically, with no loss of vitality, warmth or aliveness, and on the other hand, people who were physically in perfect health, displaying a kind of emotional deadness, apathy and emptiness.

'Being ill' engenders a sort of victim, helpless state, where we become childlike and want to be taken care of. 'Being well' demands that we're in charge of our own lives, responsible for our own actions, even despite feeling unwell or even ill.

Health is a function of many things. For emotional and mental health, participation and connection are vital. We cannot be healthy if we're disconnected from ourselves, our families, our friends, wants and needs. We need to actively participate in our lives, in our communities, in our nourishment, physically, socially, mentally and spiritually. Our bodies are an 'embodiment' of everything that is going on in our lives. What can be shocking to discover is that most of what we think is happening in our lives, is only happening in our minds, and that we're in fact disconnected from what is going on in our lives, with the people in our lives. Our lives aren't meant to be lived in our heads. Life is lived out there, with others.

Our own thinking is at the source of everything in our lives. What is the source of that thinking? What are we listening to? What words have wormed their way inside our heads?

We will all experience ill health at some stage in our lives; it's a condition of being human. We evolve in concert with our environment; we're in a constant dance with the changing circumstances of our lives. When we embrace this inevitability as part of our human condition, we can still be healthy or well despite being 'ill', if our response to the illness is a healthy response, and the way we think about our illness does not worsen the experience of the illness or lead us to take actions that aggravate the disease.

Words. Thoughts and words. It was all thoughts and words.

Were thoughts and words the source of everything? It was obvious. There wasn't anything outside of my capacity to think and express. All my thoughts and feelings occurred as words or what I couldn't express in words. Language was the water I swam in. I dived into the words.

There was no escaping the words. Words created worlds. And the world existed in words.

My existence was, and is, and will be forever, trapped in words. Could my human 'being' ever escape my human condition? What is the condition of being human?

What is the condition of being happy, or sad, lonely, right, wrong, funny, successful?

Happiness results from acceptance and letting go of what is making us unhappy. We can only create being happy in the moment. We cannot carry happiness around with us; we can just be happy when we're around. Happiness is a matter of perspective. What we see always depends on where we're looking from. When we change the way we look at things, the things we look at change.

While happiness is an emotion, love lives in communication. Where there's no loving communication, there's no love. Where there's anger, hostility, resentment and blame, there's no love present. Nor can there be happiness. Where there's acceptance, respect, understanding, forgiveness, kindness and compassion – love is present in spades. Love also only lives in the moment, out there with others. Keeping love locked up (safe) in your heart is not where love belongs. Love belongs out there, where you are. Letting love out to play is the source of a happy heart.

Self-expression is fundamental to the experience of a healthy, happy life, and fundamentally we're responsible for our own self-expression. What is the condition of being self-expressed? We all know it when we see it in others. No one can make us speak, or share, or sing, or dance. We can wilfully refuse to express (withhold) those deeply important aspects of ourselves, our vulnerability, fears, sadness, joys, desires and dreams. Or we can equally wilfully choose to express our anger, frustration, disgust, or hostility or contempt – for the benefit or detriment of others. The choice is ours. What wolf are we choosing to feed? Blaming another for "making me do it" or "stopping me from doing it" is childish and unproductive, yet we all indulge in it from time to time.

*****

Following the success of the adult diaries, I knew I wanted to do a similar diary for young people, teenagers especially, but had no idea how I'd communicate with this age group. Not having had children of my own, I felt very excluded from the understanding of a parent. However, having been a somewhat troubled young person myself, and having interacted with thousands of young people, ill and well, during my thirty-plus year medical career, I felt what might have helped me when I was growing up and trying to figure myself out might just help other young people even all these years later. The external world may change, but the internal world remains much the same. It's the internal world of thoughts and emotions and feelings and attitudes that can be so crippling. I wanted to reach in there, to interrupt some of the negative internal dialogue that could cause damage to the emerging adult.

At an event in Birmingham, I got my answer. John worked for a stationery company designing greeting cards. When I saw his drawings, I knew instantly he had a gift of communicating through pictures what was sometimes difficult to express in words.

The *Teen Diary* (now *Young Person's*) was born in 2013, and from this we developed the *Student Journal*, a *Homework Journal* for school students that we created in collaboration with the Rosses Community School in Donegal and the Department of Education in Ireland.

In 2016, we launched the *Get Up and Go Diary for Busy Women* and we also had the opportunity to work with Roger Hamilton, to create the *Genius Journal*, incorporating the tools of Wealth and Talent Dynamics with the inspirational and motivational format of the diary, as a support for all kinds of entrepreneurs. We then produced a *Gratitude Journal* and a *Daily Planner for Busy Women*. I was in my element.

I try to incorporate as much as possible of the philosophy, or way of thinking, that I've evolved over my lifetime, into the diaries each year. To me it reflects a timeless, cross-cultural, universally human wisdom, inclusive of principles or truisms that are the source of a happy and healthy life for everyone. The intention is that, on a daily basis, people can read and be present to a different perspective on life, to be aware of the choices that present each moment of each day, and how we could face a situation or a person or a problem. We all have the power to choose our actions, to design our own day, to transform our experience/perspective in any given situation, to respond rather than react. We've the opportunity, moment by moment, to consider rather than condemn, to listen rather than rush to judgement, to see life from another point of view, to be the director rather than the actor in someone else's play, to have a say in how our life goes. We're the stone, the chisel and the hand. What life are we carving?

I think our diaries makes people aware of that in a simple, yet profound and engaging way.

The day I retired, it was as if I'd gotten new 'angel wings' on my shoulders. I was free to be me, and free to play according to my inner compass. I was now engaging with new entrepreneurial communities, each of them busy trying to make the world a better place, and in a different way to my community of medical practitioners. I now had an opportunity to impact earlier and wider, to educate, inspire, motivate, encourage and empower people of all ages, from all walks of life. The world of diagnosing and treating established disease was receding for me. While my role in the relief of suffering was real and admirable, I now wanted to inhabit the world of personal empowerment and education, and the exciting and challenging world of inspiring and motivating people with words, to keep themselves well, at ease and happy, to live out the full lives they were born to live.

Ah, but who wants what I want? Who cares what I want? What do you want?

That was my next exploration.

CHAPTER 10

Where Did Heaven Go?

"I'm the way, the truth and the life; He who believes in me
will never die" – **Jesus Christ**

I started to write this book when I realised my mother was dying. Writing it was my way of dealing with the fear I had of I might die without ever have been really known.

My mother was the one person in the world who knew me better than anyone. She knew who I was, who I'd been and who I was becoming. As she began to leave me, I began to find myself. The death of a mother and the birth of a daughter. She was leaving me as her legacy. Who would I be that would honour who she was? What was I doing with the life she gave me? What could I do? What was I born to do that she didn't get to do, or couldn't do? What did she want for me? Success? Happiness? Or did she want the world to know me the way she knew me? As her daughter? Her creation? Of course she did. She was my mother and she loved me. She wanted the world to love me.

Mam was a great believer in Heaven. She always prayed a lot, not only that we would all be happy and successful in our lives, but that we would also be eternally happy in Heaven. She worried, in later years, that I might not get into Heaven, as I was divorced, so she prayed even harder.

When she was in her late eighties, and came to live with me and my then partner, she was faced with a certain reality she could no longer ignore, and berated herself slightly in colluding in the 'sin', tolerating it, not telling me to 'stop it', as if she was responsible for me getting into Heaven or not. I understood where she came from. She had grown up with a fear of God's punishment if you 'broke the rules'. Like others of her generation, she didn't distinguish between God's punishment and the priest/Church's anger or punishment. They were only afraid of what the priest told them they should be afraid of. And she was afraid of hell. And hell was where you went if you sinned.

Her fear of God's wrath came early in her life. She grew up in the countryside, outside a small town in the West of Ireland, in a small family with two sisters. There was no boy to inherit the farm or to help her dad work in the fields. Perhaps her mother wanted a better life for her daughters and encouraged them to be good in school. Mam loved school, especially the spelling test every Wednesday. When she was around seven, she misspelled FROG as FORG, and received a hard slap across both hands from the cane of the displeased teacher (who clearly expected better), which came up in two wheals.

On arriving home, her mother, seeing her two hands, asked what happened. Not wanting to incur her mother's displeasure at her poor performance in the spelling test, she said "the desk fell on my hands". Her mother, of course, bandaged her hands. She arrived in school the following day with two bandaged hands and the teacher asked her what happened. Feeling thoroughly caught, she came up with a quick solution: "I caught them in the barbed wire."

Perhaps it would've been OK if she had not been seven or in a Catholic school, or making her first Holy Communion, or the town had not been so small, or the church so near the school. But fate conspired and, as she left school that day, she saw her mother and the teacher and the priest on the steps of the church.

"That's it," she said to herself. "Two sins. Now God and the priest know. My life is over. I'm surely going straight to hell."

Not an improbable interpretation for a seven-year-old, good Catholic child from a small town in the west of Ireland in 1932, but an interpretation that possibly impacted the course of her life: "I'll never tell a lie again. I promise I'll be good. You will realise that I'm a good person, really, I am, and you will let me into Heaven."

And she was. My mum was the most gentle, sweet, compassionate, understanding mother a child could possibly have. And she valued the truth above all else. Living with the burden of lies was obviously just too painful, so we generally got to the truth of the matter pretty quickly in our house. There was never any punishment if you told the truth, no matter what it was. I never did understand how, knowing the benefit of the truth, I became such an accomplished liar. Of course, I really only lied to myself, that my lies were special – my lies were justified!

It's strange how I was so blind to my own lie; the lie I was living as if it were the truth: "I can't." The power of belief.

In her later years, after the death of my father, Mam got Sky TV. She was an intensely curious person, always interested in the world. She delighted in The Discovery Channel and all the BBC documentaries that explored the weird and wonderful natural world of monkeys and lizards and other strange creatures, and was equally fascinated by space and what existed beyond this Earth and in other galaxies. When Dad was alive, we all joked about her weird dreams, brought on by her fascination with horror and science fiction, and we all attempted to unravel their meaning at breakfast with great amusement.

One day, not long after her eightieth birthday, and about ten years after my dad's death, she said quite simply: "Where did Heaven go?"

In her rare dark moments, most frequently brought on by attempting to discontinue the anti-depressants she had been prescribed to help her cope with her grief after my dad died, she ruminated on death. In all the ever-more sophisticated documentaries and explorations of space with probes and satellites, there was no sign of Heaven. She had been so sure of it when she was a child, even a mature adult. Heaven is up there, and hell is down below and we're here. If we're good, we go to Heaven. If we're bad, we go to hell. Simple. Now what?

If there was no Heaven, where was Dad? And Ciarán – her baby who had died without having had his chance to live.

"But where am I going? I'm over eighty. I'm nearer to death than you are," she would say, "and I'm curious to know where am I going? Besides, I'm hoping that's where your dad is. I'm looking forward to meeting him again."

I got her point.

I don't have particularly fixed views of, nor do I question the reason for, my existence. I'm happy enough to find heaven on earth and generally live a pretty good life. As the product of a Christian upbringing, I choose, simply to believe in an all-merciful, compassionate, understanding God, and have an attitude of: 'I'll think about where I'm going when the time comes, but I'm probably going back where I came from.' My attitude is also: 'I wasn't too bothered before I was born so perhaps I won't be too bothered after I die. Either way, I'm here now, and that's what matters. I'll think about the afterlife later.'

Over time, Mum's cognitive function started to decline, probably through several mini strokes brought on by a lifetime of raised blood pressure.

I missed these earlier, robust conversations: they became less interesting to her, and she became more preoccupied with praying again. I felt sorry for her. Was she determined to find Heaven again? I wasn't convinced she would.

She had lived with me for almost two years, until her frailty and a succession of small strokes and a coronary event necessitated her move into a nursing home where she could receive round-the-clock care.

We had discussed this many times. Mum never wanted to be a burden on her children and had said she would like to live with me for as long as she could, and then move into a nursing home. She had been a nurse in her early years and had no fear of nursing homes, in fact almost welcoming the security and dependence on care, after a lifetime of caring for others. We regularly went to visit the nursing home where she had put her name down, but only to smile at them and say, "I'm not ready yet."

She had only been in the nursing home for six months before she died. She had gone to stay there and be with her younger sister Anne, when I went to Bali, and decided to stay. She was now back in the community in which she had grown up. Full circle. That was the beginning of the end.

I'd visit her regularly and always ask her: "So what's new? What's the craic?" And she would look around the room, at all the other frail, elderly residents, mostly sleeping or mindlessly watching the TV and say: "Sure. Where would I find any craic around here!" and laugh at her own joke.

When she moved into the nursing home, even the praying stopped. Had she given up? She was now eighty-nine, the same age her mother died. She had nothing left to do. She sat with her sister and chatted companionably about nothing in particular. Snippets of memories.

When I visited, we went through the motions of conversations. She was still the delightful, smiling, easy, loving, beautiful mother I always had, but now there wasn't anything to do. She was simply there, sitting companionably, gratefully, with her sister, her best friend by her side. A wise, happy and lucky woman, at peace with the world.

Twenty-three days after her eighty-ninth birthday, her older sister was ninety. For the occasion, I'd compiled a pictorial representation of her life: a photographic autobiography, in chronological order, of her life. I'd brought it to show it to her, and Anne, prior to presenting it to their sister, for her birthday.

There were lots of happy memories in those pages, from when we were all so much younger. All the family members and significant events were represented – from the earliest photo of the three sisters aged three, four and five years of age, to the last photo taken at Easter, three weeks earlier, aged eighty-eight, eighty-nine and almost ninety, and lots of family occasions in between. I was delighted with their reaction to the album. They were both very approving, had some great laughs at the fashion and hairstyles, and smiled fondly, remembering people who were no longer with us.

Looking through that photograph album, she saw her whole life – her school camogie days, her nursing days, her wedding to Garry, family holidays on the farm, her mother, our baby pictures, pictures from school, first Holy Communions, Confirmations, graduations, weddings, christenings, Christmas, birthdays, holidays, cousins, aunts, uncles, neighbours, a lifetime of smiles. There were beautiful memories in those pages of when we were all together and life was full of joy and sunshine and smiles and promise.

As I closed the album, saying "do you think Freda will like it?" she replied, "She will love it." Suddenly, Mam became very quiet. She looked tired. She said: "Just tell her not to wear that hat." I said: "Sure, I will." Somehow, something told me she wouldn't be telling her herself.

Then she looked at me and, in the knowing way she had, smiled and said: "I'm tired. I think I'd like to die now and go to Heaven."

"Would you?" I said, taken aback.

She paused, then said clearly: "Yes, I would."

Holding back the tears that started to well, I managed: "Well, of course, we would prefer it if you stayed here with us, but if you really want to go, we won't stop you."

And again, she smiled that wonderful, mischievous, twinkly smile of hers. I took her back to her room and helped her back into bed. She had always loved her sleep. I kissed her forehead as I normally did and said: "Bye now, I love you. See you on Wednesday."

She beamed her beautiful smile and nodded. I never saw her smile again.

She died peacefully in her sleep thirty-six hours later.

Heaven had come back for her.

I learnt afterwards that, on the Monday morning, she got up early, had breakfast and asked the nurse to dress her in something really nice. She then sent for the newspaper, which she had not read since she went into the nursing home and read it right through.

She was then visited by her nieces, daughters of the sister who had gotten the photo album the night before, and they had a great laugh about the old days. And that hat!

She phoned my brother in Canada and chatted to him and my sister-in-law for a wee while and caught up with the latest news on her grandchildren. All was well. Everyone was OK.

Her job was indeed, done. Her time was up. She was ready. Garry, the love of her life, was waiting in Heaven. Her past was calling her home.

Mam died on the 6th May, 2014.

She simply slipped away and passed over.

What happened?

I wasn't there. No one was. She left this world alone but, as she looked so peaceful, so serene, so unafraid, I imagined she saw Dad standing in the light holding out his hand and she went to greet him.

I drove the fifty miles down to the nursing home as soon as I got the news she was gone. The phone rang at ten past 2 a.m. I was awake. I had just put down an early draft of this manuscript that I was writing. Half an hour earlier, the phone downstairs had rung. I was annoyed because the phone on my bedside didn't ring. When I got to answer it, there was no one there. When I answered the phone at 2.10 a.m., the nurse said your mum passed away peacefully at 1.20 a.m. this morning. She had called to say goodbye.

When I saw her, she was lying in her bed, not moving, not breathing. She looked like she was sleeping. But her light was gone. Her smile was there but she had stopped smiling.

Where did her spark go? 'She' was no longer there. Such a mystery, this life-death interface. Life is there or it's not – no questions. No uncertainty. Alive or dead. Here or gone. No more. But something has gone somewhere – we know energy cannot be created or destroyed; it simply changes from one form to another. The ultimate mystery of life: where do we come from and where do we go? Who or what is this 'we', this 'I', that is there one minute and gone the next?

My mother died in May, her favourite month, in her eighty-ninth year.

She had always asked that we make sure the *Queen of the May* would be sung at her funeral. It was.

We had made a trip to Medjugorje when she was eighty-three. We were a group of twenty friends, and three of us had our mothers with us, all in their eighties! We were accompanied by our own singer-guitarist, Mike, who entertained us in the evenings after dinner.

It was a wonderful trip, but the highlight for my mum was when Mike played and sang *Queen of the May* in the huge Basilica on Sunday morning. The joy on her face was priceless.

"Dear Lady, we crown you with blossoms today

Queen of the Angels and Queen of the May".

Thank you, God – her prayers were answered: a happy life and a peaceful death.

But where did she go? I say she didn't go far. And she left something important after her: me.

Now my question was, what was I left here for? What contribution would I make to the world that would acknowledge and credit her as my mother? What difference did I want to make? I listened. What was my heart saying?

"Have patience," it said.

And I heard again those wise words she lovingly spoke: "Mind yourself, Eileen. Everything will work out just fine."

I say we all pass into the next breath of someone who speaks our name with love.

And why are we here anyway? To do what? Suffer and cause more suffering, or live in a way that moves humanity forward, one loving word at a time. We can make mischief or we can make amends. We get to choose. We have a voice, a powerful tool. We have a say in how life goes. We have a say in how our world turns out.

We get to choose. We get to say. We have a voice. We have a say in the matter of how our lives, and the world, go. Don't die with your music (your voice, your truth) inside you.

CHAPTER 11

Forgiving My Prison Guards

*"We cannot discover new oceans unless we have the
courage to lose sight of the shore"* – **André Gide**

The Sum of All Our Yesterdays

'Your life today is the sum total of all your yesterdays.'

Yep. That about sums it up. We're the pinnacle of our achievements,
we're the nadir (the lowest and most unsuccessful part) of our
journey, and everywhere in between, on the way up or on the way
down, depending on how we view what we see, when we look around
us. Often, however, our mind's eye is not satisfied with what our eyes
see. Our mind is way ahead. Our mind is focused on trying to figure
out where we're going – and how we're going to get there. In our
mind, are we looking to the ground or to the stars? To the familiar
past or the uncertain future? The mind does not like uncertainty. We
must choose the direction of our gaze. What got us here is obvious.
We inherited certain circumstances and capacities. We made certain

choices. We took certain actions. We made the best of what we were given. And here we are, after all our yesterdays.

So, what of tomorrow? Is it inevitable it will be much like yesterday? For some of us, yes. Especially if we're comfortable where we are and do the same things today that we did yesterday. But what about for those of us who aren't comfortable, who wonder how we got here, what happened? Those who think this is not how it's meant to be, who want tomorrow to be different?

But how can it be different? Because of the gift of today. Today is happening right now. Tomorrow has not yet happened. We can do something today that will guarantee that tomorrow is not like yesterday. We can design the tomorrow of our choice by our actions today. We can book an appointment, arrange to meet a friend, write a letter, apply for a place on that workshop, start to research a new opportunity, change our attitude from one of resignation and hopelessness to one of gratitude and optimism, stop listening to the negativity, start listening for encouragement.

We can start right now. This minute. We can raise our gaze from the ground upward towards a bright future, one we can now see, simply because we're looking.

The Power of Words

Are you trapped in a sentence from your past?

"In the beginning was the Word, and the word was with God, and the Word was God". It's all words. Everything ever written: words, trapped on a page, including the Bible itself. Stories trapped, but there to liberate. And all our words start from the same place: ourselves.

Spoken or written, we're the source. We chose the words we let out of our mouth.

"You can shoot me, you can jail me, but you cannot make me speak". Indeed.

Only I can do that. What words will liberate you? Who will utter them? Who spoke them into existence in the first place?

What word will set you free? Was it courage that liberated me, the courage to say "Now"?

We live our lives in the shadow of six words: Why? What? Who? When? Where? How? Why am I here? What is my life for? Who am I anyway? When will I die? Where am I going? How will I know?

Where do we expect the answers will come from? Somewhere else? Someone else? My question is, if it's your life, who should I ask? Whose answer would you accept? Your answers are right there, on the tip of your tongue, if you are willing to say it. We so want to default to "I don't know", as if that's a valid excuse. Of course, we don't know. That's life. It hasn't happened yet. You can say anything. "In the beginning was the Word...". We get to make it up as we go along.

Where are you? Here?

What time is it? Now?

Why are you here? To shine.

How do I do that? Just be here. Now.

What do you want?

Aha – that's the question!

Since the dawn of writing on cave walls, we've captured our thoughts in words: the curse and the gift of language, the liberation and entrapment of our words. Words, on stone, on paper, on our tongues, in our minds. Trillions of words, in billions of sentences, in millions of conversations, in thousands of forms, in hundreds of languages, spoken by countless identities, in tens of generations, in two genders, in one species, on one planet. All the ideas and the sentiments, the imagined thoughts, the dreams, facts, fiction, fantasy, proof, evidence, opinions, inventions, concepts, explanations, interpretations, stories, the imaginary, the suggestions, the descriptions, the evidence and the creations. Surely we should know all the answers by now?!

What is the question?

What are all the words for? To be read, listened to, and used, as fuel to help us get what we want.

Why do we listen? To be enlightened, educated or to understand? Or to justify, explain, prove, judge, condemn?

All the words that were ever written, or spoken, were done so in order to be read or heard, and to make a difference. Some belong to another time. The earth is no longer flat.

We need new words to create new evolutions and revolutions. We need new words to inspire and encourage and lead the way. A new enlightened language for a new enlightened human being. No longer trapped in the stories of the past, we can be liberated to create newly.

As human beings we have words – we can create anything in language. Words have awesome power both to create and destroy.

We can create mischief by throwing them like stones into glass houses, or pain by withholding the ones that others long to hear. We can make amends by speaking with love and compassion.

Whose mouth are they coming out of?

A Meaning Worthy of My Life

I consider myself exceptionally lucky that I had the opportunity, the courage and the willingness to embark on a new career in publishing while I was still a practising anaesthetist, before I retired from my medical career.

I'm all about self-expression, and aware that it's my responsibility. No one can express me – only me. I discovered for myself the power of my words to transform my own life. Now I'm tasking myself to transform the lives of others who are willing to listen. I'd already unknowingly been sharing my wisdom and insight naturally with people – not fully realising not everyone thought as I did or could see what I saw. I was always grateful for the opportunity to inspire, and delighted when someone left the conversation encouraged with a new perspective and a feeling of optimism. I heard the term 'to inspire' defined as "to breathe new life into" – that takes speaking, and listening, and speaking. Something magical always transpires in the miracle of dialogue.

My grandfather and my father are dead and silent in the grave. My mother is with them 'in Heaven'. All their words still live, through me. While I'm alive, I've tasked myself to continue to speak as they would have wanted me to speak – for love and understanding, kindness and compassion, justice and fairness, hope and humility, peace and freedom, for civic duty and personal responsibility. They didn't speak so much of 'happiness'. Contentment may be a pearl of greater value. Acceptance is the key that unlocks many doors.

Now that I've 'freed' my voice from the constraints of my 'stoppage' and liberated myself in the process, I'm free to create a future of my choice, guided by my words. People chained to their past, unwilling to let go, unwilling to forgive, resentful and judgemental, justified and righteous, will never experience peace in the present moment, nor the freedom to create a new future. Only by letting go of the monkey bars behind you, are you free to reach for those in front of you.

In my career as a doctor, I've seen many people die. I've witnessed the moment that a person ceases to be alive, when the light goes out, the breathing stops, the heart slows to a standstill, the spirit leaves – and it's all over.

Why do people always notice the peace that is visible on the faces of the dead as they lie in the coffin? They've let everything go; all they had carried from the past, all the cares and worries they carried round with them, as if a noose, invisible, but the strain clearly visible on their face, in their eyes, worn down and exhausted from carrying a heavy burden. Death is truly a liberation from our mortal coil. We're born mortal, but who applies the coil?

I now know that peace is possible for us in life, for those of us who say we want it. There's no path to peace, peace IS the way. It requires each of us to be peaceful in the moment, in the mind. Peace of mind is the ultimate goal. We don't have to wait until we die. We're presented with choices – every minute of every day. We can choose to be peaceful. We can choose to be happy. We can choose to love. We just need to let go of what robs the moment of this possibility. This takes giving up knowing that we think we already know; giving up our cynicism and our resignation; letting go of doubt and while nothing is certain, everything is possible. I know that now. You must discover it for yourself.

Nelson Mandela said in his autobiography, *Long Walk to Freedom*: "If I don't forgive my prison guards, I'll forever be their prisoner." I had to forgive my prison guard. I thought it was my mother I needed to forgive. It wasn't. It was me. I put myself in a prison of my own making. My freedom came the day I summoned the courage to tell my mum the truth about what I'd 'discovered' about myself.

Why did this take so much courage? Firstly, I had to dig deep. It was so parked away in my subconscious, I was unaware of any need to apologise for anything, let alone forgive. Somehow, uncovering my past from the perspective of years, as an adult, my story didn't sound like such an accurate or realistic interpretation of the events at the time. Understandable, but clearly faulty.

There were a lot of tears, and laughs, that day. I apologised for taking my love and trust away from her. I simply had to forgive myself and have compassion for that upset six-year-old, on top of the hurt three-year-old.

As if by some miracle, all the love and trust flooded back in an instant, and the vague shadowy darkness in my chest that had haunted me for years in my mind's eye, became a warm pink, as the hole in my heart healed over. I was now 'whole', full of love, and overflowing with gratitude. I got my mum back: I'd let my mother's love back into my heart and into my life, and I was now free to give it away. I was filled with inexplicable joy. I was home.

Another line from Nelson Mandela's book: "What good is my freedom if all around me are still in chains?" Releasing myself from my 'prison' left me free in life: at peace with the world. Sharing it with my mother also released her, from the prison her 'guilt' had sentenced her to.

I now want to share this with everyone, as an access for whoever else wants it. I speak for the possibility of freedom to be and peace of mind for everyone, because this is what matters to me. If I don't speak, and stay silent, I'm withholding something valuable, and that is not who I am. I'm courageous, self-expressed and a stand for all people knowing peace is possible.

Chapter 12

Learning to Let Go with Love

*"No one can go back to the past and create a new beginning, but anyone can start here and create a new ending." – **Mary Robinson.***

I struggled to complete the final chapters in this book, as the new life I was creating suddenly started to unravel. This chapter was particularly difficult to write, and while I may have preferred to leave it out, fearing the consequences of causing further upset, omitting it could leave a hole in my 'memoir' and might also demonstrate a lack of courage on my part. Fear could not be the reason to leave out an important part of my story and its lessons. Courage would have to prevail.

While I endeavour to share my experience of what happened, and how I came to make the choices I made, I am aware that there are other players in the story of my life, each of whom are also worthy of honest and respectful portrayal, and it is not my wish to cause any harm, or unintentional upset to anyone, with my words.

This chapter has now been included, both as evidence of my promise to speak with the courage, integrity and honesty I value, and to own up and admit to my own 'blind spots'. I am now aware of how fear, lack of courage and miscommunication significantly impacted the most important relationship of my life.

Until this pivotal point, I had considered myself most fortunate in my choice of life and business partner. We met on a 12-day, arduous fundraising trip to Everest Base Camp in November 2002. He had been a last-minute entrant on the team in place of a friend. He was an instant hit with the group with his easy charm, and understated, modest nature. With his natural physical strength and obvious ability, he generously helped the weaker and less experienced trekkers like myself. At the same time, he brought fun and good humour, keeping everyone's spirits up when the going got tough.

It was these qualities of humility, support, generosity, fun and caring that I was attracted to. At the end of that extraordinary adventure, I acknowledged the pleasure and privilege of having had an opportunity to get to know him and to share such a unique experience. I was not long out of an disappointing marriage, so I was reluctant to set any expectations regarding embarking on a new relationship. I considered myself extremely lucky to have met him, and valued his friendship. He was separated, with three grown-up children still living at home. Over the next few years our relationship developed naturally, and he moved in to live with me in 2008. By this time, he had also joined me in the company. Life was great and getting better. I would proudly declare when asked that "I did have to go to the top of the world to meet him."

I was still working in my local hospital, while quietly growing our diary business. I fully embraced the opportunity to develop the potential of the diaries. We were building a powerful global platform on which to freely share the wisdom of the ages, as an encouragement for everyone to live a life they loved.

For years I had immersed myself in a world of "anything is possible" with communication. I had brought myself to a place in my life where I felt could confidently encourage others to confront their fears and overcome their challenges. I was now fully participating in life with a new-found freedom of expression and relishing the opportunity to make a difference in the world, with words – words that would hopefully inspire and encourage others to explore their own barriers to self-expression.

We got engaged in Bali in 2013 and were due to get married in June 2015.

Suddenly, life threw a curveball. Nothing had prepared me for what was to come. I was blindsided.

In February 2015, four months before our planned wedding, an emotional 'bomb' went off in my life, in our relationship, in the middle of the kitchen, on a Friday afternoon, with the words, "Sit down. I have something to tell you." What followed was an admission that my partner of 13 years had another family: a son and a daughter, from another relationship, and this daughter, now 26, was dying in a palliative care ward in a city hospital.

Impossibly, two of his daughters had been critically ill, in the same hospital, at the same time, with the same condition, two wards apart. While one daughter, whom I knew and loved, was thankfully recovering from a particularly severe and life-threatening episode – during which we had spent three days and nights by her bedside, willing her to live – the other girl was in the next ward, on a palliative regime. She died two days later.

I was stunned. I realised, of course, that this was a massive personal tragedy for my partner, and my heart broke for him on the loss of his daughter. However, the shock for me was that I'd never heard of this person! In our 13 years together, he had never mentioned this girl. No one in his family had ever spoken of her to me. I was bewildered. The ground I thought I stood on disappeared from under me.

Devastated for the man I loved, on the death of his obviously beloved daughter, I was shocked at the enormity of the realisation of his apparent capacity to withhold such an important aspect of his life from me. I felt hurt and betrayed. I had trusted him with my life. What could I trust now? I felt like I had been thrown into an ocean of emotion without a life raft, and I was drowning.

So many questions. What should I do? Why did he choose not to tell me? Why would he want to keep her a secret from me? I couldn't imagine what his family must have thought, assuming that I knew. Did they assume I didn't want to speak about these children or acknowledge their existence – for 13 years?! Did his family think I was such a judgemental person? Did they know me at all? Does anybody truly know anybody?

Not knowing how to deal with this emotional and tragic situation, my brain took over. The event had triggered a memory of an earlier betrayal – a breach of trust – and my reaction was a familiar response: I'm suffering and it's your fault. I reverted to attack! – to punish. The predictable response to a familiar upset; a 'brain pattern', an automatic reaction to a perceived betrayal. I reacted the way I did when I was six. Hurt and confused, I 'broke the doll' in anger and frustration: go away, I hate you. I can't trust you. I don't need you. You lied to me!

But I wasn't saying it to my mother this time, but to my partner with whom I'd shared my life for 13 years. Nor was I saying it out loud; this screamed silently in the prison of the unsaid.

I attended the funeral in support of the man I loved and had shared so much of my life with, and planned to deal with my new reality later. The funeral was one of the saddest I'd ever attended. She was 26 and obviously a beautiful and much-loved girl. I felt deprived of the privilege of having known her. She would've been 13 in 2002. Her father was utterly heartbroken. My heart broke for him, while it was also breaking for myself, and my own shattered illusions about the man I thought I knew, the life I thought we had shared and the future we had been planning.

I didn't imagine I could possibly know what it would be like to lose a child, and how he would be affected and how it would impact the relationship, but I knew there was trouble ahead. I'd witnessed grief too many times during my medical career, yet always at a distance. A certain empathetic detachment was usually called for in breaking bad news to patients, especially parents. I didn't have a personal experience of loss to this degree in any of my friends or family. A dear friend was 57. Dad was 76. Mam was 89. 'The old must go'. It's sad but seems natural somehow. Not so with the young.

I wanted to be strong for him, and for myself.

We still had a future.

Or did we?

Some small awareness of the inconsolability of grief was triggered in me as a part of a 'remembered' grief – witnessing the effect on my mother at losing her baby when I was three. No matter what I did or said at that time, nothing made any difference for her. Despite my protestations of "mammy, mammy, please don't cry, I'm here", she was lost in her grief. It seemed that nothing could compensate for the loss.

And there I was, 55 years later, losing the love of my life as he was losing himself in grief at the loss of his precious child; another 'baby' I had never met.

Could our relationship be saved?

He expressed regret that he had not told me about her. He explained that he was "afraid" to tell me "for fear I would leave". That left me equally bewildered. Did he really think I was that kind of person? Had I ever said anything to have him believe that might be true?

He insisted he had tried to tell me once, but I had said: "I don't want to know". I remembered the occasion, and had assumed I knew what he was trying to tell me – so I reassured him if it was in the past, it probably wasn't that important!

He didn't contradict me.

Maybe he was relieved and simply took me at my word, and justified his silence believing it to be for the greater good?

My mistake was thinking I knew what he was trying to tell me.

His mistake was not trying harder.

We think we know people!

Anyway, now that I knew, what would I do? I was in a painful dilemma. I felt betrayed yet trapped. If I left, his fear would be justified. If I stayed, I was staying with a man who had kept an important aspect of himself, and his life, hidden from me, and unwittingly had betrayed my trust and broken my heart.

Could I stay in this relationship? Could I trust him again?

In uncharted waters, I retreated into my own thoughts, as did he. When we should have been sharing our mutual pain, we tried to deal with our individual pain, separately. I needed some reassurance that I could trust him again, but he was too blinded by grief to consider my needs.

I decided to get to work on creating new possibilities for myself and the relationship. I created the possibility of being accepting and forgiving. The past was the past. It couldn't be changed. I was still committed to creating a future; a great life. I'd always said that anything and everything was forgivable. Now I was being tested.

We had an opportunity to meet an Irish priest visiting from the US, Fr Gerry O'Rourke, and we had a profound conversation about forgiveness. I knew if there was any future for us, I needed to forgive. The challenge, however, was to forgive him totally, completely, absolutely and unconditionally.

Could I do that?

Being the person I am, and wanting the man I believed my partner was, and wanting the future and the relationship I wanted, I figured that, yes, I'd be willing to forgive him. He made a mistake. We're all human, and we make mistakes. And, like the rest of us, he had his many redeeming and endearing qualities – kindness, thoughtfulness and all that he had lovingly and generously contributed to my life, both personally and in our business, over many years. So, yes, he was deserving of forgiveness and I was deserving of freedom, so, yes, I forgave him. I forgave him totally, completely and absolutely.

But was it unconditionally?

I knew I needed to forgive myself – for my mistake, for stepping over what I had stepped over, for not listening, for all I had turned a blind eye to, for fear of what I could lose, and, finally, throwing the toys out of the cot and reacting like an upset six-year-old, hurt again by the perceived betrayal of the one who said they loved me.

I wondered: did he also need to forgive himself? I felt that without this, my forgiveness would be insufficient. If we didn't mutually forgive each other, and ourselves, what hope did we have?

I also wanted a 'better' explanation; one I could understand. Fearing I would leave didn't make sense to me, yet had that same fear stopped me from listening when he tried to speak?

I believed, with time, and open and honest disclosure, we'd make sense of everything.

I waited ...

He showed a brave face to the world as he carried on his work. He shared openly with others about his grief and his loss and his fears for the health of his other daughter. At home, he was doing everything he knew to do, to try to make it up to me. Everything but talk. Somehow it felt to me that he believed he could never make it up to me, that he would never be forgiven.

I wanted us to get on with our lives and create a new future. Was he terrified of the future? How could he create a future with me when the only future he could see was a reminder of the past with all its pain?

He retreated into his grief and I was unable to reach him. I felt excluded and alone. Not being a mother kept me somewhat insulated from the depth of the pain he was feeling – but also kept me at arm's length as someone who couldn't possibly understand.

I carried on carrying on. I had forgiven him. I loved him. I'd invested so much in our relationship. We were business partners. We shared a vision of the future. I believed what we had was special, and I wanted it back. I didn't want it to be an illusion.

For me, it was like the solid foundation on which we had built our relationship had turned to sand and shifted under my feet, but I was still committed to making it work. I wanted a new foundation upon which we could build a new future. What could that be?

I needed a promise I could trust.

So, I waited ... for something. Some conversation where a new promise would be declared. Some reassurance there would be no more secrets. Some 'miracle' that would restore my trust and confidence that we could get past this into the possibility of a bright future.

Four years went by ...

And no miracle came. No magic words to make it all better.

And the days rolled on. No real dialogue; a reluctance to revisit old wounds, to reach an understanding, a way to put it all behind us. I craved a sign that I could trust the foundation we were building, that we had cleared up the mess, had each accepted responsibility for our part, and he had restored the honour of his word to me – a word I could again rely on; a word we could both honour in a marriage vow; a word that meant what it said.

The silence was deafening.

The chasm got wider. 'Whatever you say, say nothing'. 'Least said, soonest mended'. Tick-tock. Groundhog Day.

I was at the end of knowing what to do or where to go. I was stuck. Something was still missing for me. What was it? Trust? Truth?

We were still engaged, but I didn't feel I had gotten to the point where I could confidently exchange a wedding vow. I was worried that if he had kept such a secret so well, what other secrets might he be capable of keeping? Could I ever trust him with my heart again, really?

That was a question only I could answer.

I needed to do something radical to break the deadlock. I took a risk, declared the engagement over and returned his ring.

He moved out in March 2019, a month before my 60th birthday.

We continued to work together, although it was difficult.

Six months passed slowly.

I dealt with the breakdown the only way I knew how: I talked to people. I shared my upset. I reached out to others for support. I had to trust my mother's words, that "everything would turn out for the best".

On the day I returned from a nine-day 'spiritual' Journey of Lights Tour, having visited India, Nepal and Tibet, (in the footsteps of Gandhi, Buddha and the Dalai Lama), 17 years to the week when we first met on that trek to Everest Base Camp, and eight months since I had given back the ring, he told me he was in a new relationship. He told me he had "moved on" and suggested I do the same. There would be no conversation about reconciliation.

I busied myself and tried to stop questioning what had happened. I defaulted to asking if it was all my fault? In affairs of the heart, was I just a distrustful person, waiting to be betrayed? Was this going to be the never-ending theme in the story of my life?

I looked back into those early years.

I had made an unconscious 'decision' at six years of age (following my tonsillectomy) that I couldn't trust anyone who said they loved me, figuring it was just a trick to let other people hurt you. My mother had told me I was going on my holidays. She lied. She said she loved me. I trusted her. They hurt me and she let them. She betrayed me. I decided, "Don't trust people who say they love you!"

Settled into my subconscious, it wasn't a problem for most of my teenage years. In fact, it probably protected me from a lot of that teenage angst. I accepted I wasn't popular with boys. too quiet and shy, I didn't see myself as attractive in any way, and definitely not girlfriend material, so I simply concentrated on my studies and was grateful for the friendship of a few close girl friends.

When I did progress to boyfriends in college, and early adulthood, any mention of the word 'love' was enough for me to run. That was 'danger' territory; that's where the potential for real hurt was. I sought out 'safe' relationships where there wasn't much declaration or demonstration of love, and got comfortable. Everything would be going OK, until the love word came up, and I'd have to escape. I dated some really lovely guys, and had a few long-term relationships in which I really wanted to be committed, but only until the dreaded love word was mentioned. I couldn't understand it.

I had long forgotten the upset six-year-old's decision about life and the world, and began to doubt my capacity to love at all. I struggled to know what 'love' was. I read books and magazines that talked about love, but how do you KNOW you love someone – enough to trust them? Which came first – love or trust? I was waiting to 'feel' it and, when I didn't feel it, I thought I was safe, as long as I didn't have to say it, and lie because I didn't feel it. So, when they said it, I was upset. I couldn't say it. So, I would leave the relationship. I had the most delightful boyfriend in college; that relationship came to an abrupt end when there was a hint at possible marriage down the line. A few years later, I was engaged to another lovely man, but panicked six weeks before I was due to get married, and broke it off.

Predictably, my wonderful parents supported me, saying it was better to be sure before than regret after.

I was bereft. I didn't know what was 'wrong' with me. I thought I was normal enough. I loved the company of men, and I thought I loved my fiancé, but I just didn't know what this 'love' was when they said I 'love' you. How could I trust it was true? And so I never said it. To anyone. I tried it, but it sat like sand in my mouth; a dead word. Something was missing, and I didn't know what it was.

After the break-up of my engagement, I ran away to Australia. The day I should have been walking down the aisle, I was on a Qantas direct flight from London to Sydney. I was elated: I had escaped! My friend had a huge farm and I took refuge in a caravan at the bottom of her garden and contemplated my life. What was I doing? What did I want?

I busied myself herding sheep on horseback, picnicking in the outback, languishing in the warm sunshine until I realised, after several weeks of hiding, I couldn't stay there, in my friend's garden, at the other side of the world, living in a corner of someone else's life. I knew I had to go back, face the music, my friends, family, colleagues, and face the man I had been in a relationship with for five years and had so obviously hurt, and his friends and family. I left Australia, Then I left my job in Scotland and returned home to Ireland. It was hard to face the reality of what I had done.

As soon as I got home, I did the only thing I knew to do – I stopped talking. I simply didn't know what I could say that would be the truth. Rather than pretend or lie, I simply went silent. This was strangely liberating for me, but so upsetting for my parents. They worried. They sent for my friends. Everyone tried to get me to speak. To no avail. What could I say? More of the same? I couldn't tell people what I was feeling or thinking, because I didn't know what I was feeling or thinking. If I didn't speak then I didn't risk anything. And I could suffer in silence. I had caused so much suffering – better be silent in myself and not make matters worse. Or was it better? I didn't even know that. Again, I was trapped. In silence, again; self-imposed silence.

I think I stayed silent for about six weeks.

Then I stopped being silent and started talking.

Everyone was relieved; especially me. I don't remember why I stopped, or how I stopped. I just stopped not talking and started again. It was time.

I apologised to my fiancé. I apologised to my friends and family. I comforted myself in my work.

Then I met someone else. He swept me off my feet. I really thought I was in love this time. We got engaged.

We got married.

We travelled the world.

It didn't work out.

We got divorced.

I was right – you can't trust people who say they love you.

That was the point at which I realised I had to confront my past. It was time to stop running away from my mother. It was time to tell her I loved her. I'm sorry. Please forgive me. I love you. My heart opened. I came home; the hurt was healed.

Then I went on the trip of a lifetime – 12 days in the Himalayas on a fundraising trek to Everest Base Camp.

This time it would be different.

I knew I could now trust a person who said they loved me.

I knew what love was – and that it was all in the declaration.

I knew that it took courage to tell people that you loved them.

I know that knowing makes no difference.

Perhaps Shakespeare was right: "There's a divinity that shapes our ends, rough hew them how we will".

Some months later, he gave another explanation – the reason he kept his daughter a secret from me was because he had promised her that he would never tell me about her!

I heard what he said. It didn't make it any easier for me. He had given his word to a 13-year-old girl, 17 years earlier.

Was it all about courage? Was he simply trapped between a rock and a hard place? It takes courage to tell the truth. Fearing the loss of love, did he have a choice? Who should you choose? Not wanting to lose either of us, it seems like he lost both.

So, now I knew.

But it was all too late.

He had moved on.

He was in a new relationship. He was happy. He was optimistic about the future.

It hit me. Yes, it was my doing – I just hadn't quite planned for that finality.

Was this what I wanted for him? To be happy?

I had set him free. He was free to be in a relationship without the burden of a secret. He had the peace of mind he craved. She was a lucky girl. She had the free man I'd wanted all along.

They say: "If you love them, let them go. If they are for you, they will return. If they don't, they were never yours."

And me? What would I do?

Could I now forgive him for moving on? Yes, I could. And I did.

He is a good person. He deserves to be happy. He has all those special qualities I admired. We shared many happy times. He simply chose to withhold something about himself from me, thinking, or hoping, it wouldn't harm the relationship, while at the same time perhaps terrified it would.

Was that understandable? Yes.

Was it his right to choose? Of course.

Did it work for our relationship? No.

In my understanding, keeping secrets, withholding important aspects of ourselves, is not conducive to an intimate and loving relationship. Sharing is important. Sharing builds trust. Lying and pretending leaves people guarded for fear of discovery, unavailable for intimacy. Keeping secrets, hiding who we are, living in fear of being found out, damage relationships and causes unnecessary suffering. We must risk being ourselves, with all our vulnerabilities. We must trust that we're loving, lovable and loved.

I had to be willing to let go of the past and to forgive, both myself and him, for all of it. I had to have compassion, for both of us. I had to own, and be willing to deal with, the consequences of my choice.

Of course I wanted to hide. I was raw, and vulnerable. Here was yet another failed relationship for which I had to accept my part. I was facing a future alone, without my partner and my best friend. He was still my business partner and we were committed to having a respectful professional relationship and a successful global business. I had a life to live. I had to get out and engage with people. I was in the business of 'inspiring and motivating people'.

I chose to continue to show up in the outside world as myself; someone who could, and would, courageously dust myself off, and get up and go again.

I moved on. I would deal with my upset, disappointment and failure in my own way. I found a space in which I could express everything that needed to be expressed, and also acknowledge myself for all my efforts. I had to allow myself to grieve my loss and remain loving and forgiving. I had to complete that part of my life to make space for something new.

Perhaps I stayed four years longer than I should have done, thinking there was an answer that would make it all go away – and we could get back to normal – trying to ignore the obvious, put off the inevitable, avoid the reality that the damage was done, and it was irreparable. Did I think he would change? Yes, I did. I thought I knew him. Do we ever truly know anyone? We spend a lifetime trying to figure out ourselves – it is arrogant to think we can know another human being, beyond what they let us know.

Love is indeed blind, and deaf, and occasionally dumb.

So, yes, it looks like I reacted to a perceived betrayal by "throwing the toys out of the cot", only it wasn't sudden. I wasn't six. I wasn't confused. This time I was an adult. This time I was choosing. I left the relationship because I needed to stand up for the values I hold so dear – integrity and responsibility. I needed to shine in my own truth.

I do not see either of us as victim, or helpless, or powerless or wronged. This is simply what happened as a result of a choice. It is often said, "We are free to choose but we are not free from the consequences of our choice". I was free to choose, and chose powerfully, not from fear, but from love, and I accepted responsibility for the consequences of that choice. It takes courage to tell the truth. It takes courage to face the uncertain future.

I had to let go of the illusion of a future I had planned for one that is about to show up. I now have the freedom and peace of mind that comes with letting go, to allow a future I know nothing about, but one where there is still the possibility of shining in the art of living.

I'm now free of the eight-year-old in the fawn coat who got trapped in the 'hated' Eileen Forrestal – liberated from her coat of armour designed by a lonely and scared six-year-old, as a defence to help her survive the hurts of the world. I'm now a responsible adult, who completed an important relationship, one for which she is forever grateful, that allowed her to learn so much about herself, to grow and develop as a person, and to discover what it takes to be a novice in the exploration of one's own humanity.

Forgiveness is key to everything.

CHAPTER 13

Claiming My Voice

"Your playing small does not serve the world"
– Marianne Williamson

The Courage to Shine

The courage to shine, the message being: it takes courage to show up and be seen as the stars we are, the loving, twinkling souls that shine from our happy eyes. Everything else is a smokescreen, a mask to hide the pain of not being understood.

We're mostly sleepwalking through life, or 'sleep-talking', anaesthetising ourselves from the pain of the reality that 'this is it'! We're hypnotising ourselves with lies and deceptions, innocently absorbing a diet of fairy tales and princesses and magic wands and happy ever afters that tell us 'this is not it'. We're telling ourselves there's a better time, and a better life, someday, out there, in the future – my prince will come, on a white horse and whisk me away to the land of happy ever after!

I spent twenty years as an anaesthetist putting people to sleep and, every day, multiple times a day, called out to people to "wake up, it's time to wake up" to rouse them from their drug-induced state. Now I say: "Awaken from your word-induced sleep. Stop waiting, listening to the lies that say you have time. Face the fears that keep you paralysed, small, silent and hidden. Deal with that negative internal voice that says you can't, that you're not ready, that you're not good enough. And start speaking the truth of who you are, really, and have the courage to ask for what you want in your life, right now. Go for what will make your heart sing!" We have language. We have the power to cause anything. Words are as powerful (and as lethal) as drugs! We need to wake up to the realisation and responsibility of this.

Now is the only time to wake up. There's no operation to get over, no 'later'. This is it; you are missing your life. Wake up, it's happening now! The operation IS your life. This is the time to be happy. This is the time to be healthy and well, confident, powerful, grown-up and responsible, doing what it takes to have your life work, and the world work. This is the time to be the shining light you were born to be.

It starts with the willingness, the willingness to consider that perhaps, in fact, you could be asleep. It takes courage to open your eyes to what's happening in your life, to wake up when all around are sleeping, to face the truth of who you are and how your life is. You will not be thanked for waking the others, who are trying to sleep, exhausted as they toss and turn on their bed of nails. SSSSSSSHHHHHHHHH!!!! They hiss angrily. You may have to face ridicule, cynicism, rejection, punishment for daring to disturb the status quo, the accepted norm, the comfort of agreement. "We are ALL TRYING TO SLEEP!!"

These are all aspects of fear, if the truth be known: the fear of the unknown. To avoid the void of the unknown tomorrow we fill it with the familiar stuff of yesterday. If that worked, why are we upset when things don't go the way we planned? Why do we wait for something to happen then complain that it happened? Why do we do things that have clear consequences and then act bewildered by the consequences? Is it the responsibility we fear – that we will have to own the unknown outcome of our actions? Is that why we take the same tried and trusted actions over and over, the ones that 'worked' once upon a time in the past, yet wanting and expecting a different result? No wonder people are upset all the time. We think there is a place called the future and, in the future, everything will be different, or better, certainly better than now, if only we could get there. But were always here. Here is the point of power. Here is where it's at. What keeps the individual from realising their true power in this world – in the present moment – of speaking up with truth with courage and confidence, doing what needs to be done to create a life and a world worthy of our presence?

Where do we lose our power? It starts with the simple things. We sit quietly in school and learn what the teachers and parents want us to know. We do what we're told: be good, nice, be seen and not heard, don't ask stupid (**difficult**) questions. There's a threat of being punished for going outside the rules, of being banished. No one will want you or listen to you; you will be mocked and ostracised. And so, to avoid that shame of that fate, you learn to live a life of quiet desperation, trying to fit in and belong, staying safe. Some are brave souls. They rebel. They are punished. And so you wait, in the shadows, hoping you will be discovered, or released, before it's too late, before you give up. Your soul's small voice, the one you came here to express, wants a chance to shine. Little by little, you lose your confidence, your courage fails, you resign yourself cynically, if not hopelessly, to your fate, your small soul's voice drowned out by the constant noise of the world telling you who you should or shouldn't be, and you snuff out your own light.

Yes, it takes courage. It takes courage to speak your truth, to admit your fears. It also takes courage to listen. It's challenging to listen. We have to confront our prejudices. We have to be willing to see the world from another point of view which may be at loggerheads with our own. What we hear may challenge our world view, and we may have to change our view– from the familiar one we're comfortable with to an entirely new one. Where does that leave our identity? With a different view of life, are we now different?

Following my 'breakthrough' at the microphone, yes, people saw me as different to how I had been before. I behaved differently. I said different things to what they were used to. This confused them slightly. For myself, I felt like an entirely new person, and yet I was exactly as I'd always known myself to be. Not everyone liked the new me. They preferred me with my stories and complaints and judgements, with my righteous justifications, my drama and upsets. This loving, self-expressed, happy and confident person, suddenly newly excited by life, seemed somehow to discombobulate them. Somehow, did my transformation occur as a threat? If I could change so radically, and so easily, what about them?

No one can change us but ourselves, and only if we want to. We can change our clothes and our hairstyle, our job, our partner, our environment, yet we remain unchanged. I realised this with all my efforts to escape. I wanted to change the world. When I couldn't change the world, I tried to change my job, or country. It never worked. It never occurred that I could possibly change myself. Who would I change myself into? Every time I looked in the mirror I was there! I needed to change the lens I was looking through. Looking through a different lens can alter who we perceive ourselves to be. It challenges us to consider an alternative view. In this instance, I dared to look beyond the limits of my own view of myself, to step beyond the boundaries of my past, to create and express who I wanted to be in the present, who I was anyway before I had to change myself to fit in and survive my own story. I am now free to shine my own light. Yes, I can see how that might occur as a threat to the identity of others.

So, am I changed? Or have I simply been returned to myself? Did my inner listener seek out the voice that spoke to my heart's desire? Did I get an opportunity to listen to other words, see another view and accept it as valid? When my mother confided in me that, forty years after my 'accident', I had finally become the person she hoped I would be when I was three, I knew I had come home to me. "In your heart, you know".

We have a voice – it's a powerful tool. We can make words that make worlds – real or illusionary – we tell the truth, or we lie, and both contribute to the world we create. If you have a life you love, or a life you want to escape from, know that you created it. Every choice you made, every turn your life took, got you here. This is the life you made for yourself. If you created that, what else can you create? Can you create the life of your dreams? Only if you want to. What if you were the author of your future life?

Perhaps we need to learn how to use the gift of language more powerfully and creatively. The point of power is always in the present moment. The secret to life is to live powerfully in the present moment.

We have free speech – but consider we have a lot to learn by listening.

With freedom comes responsibility

Do we tell the truth, or do we lie? Perhaps we learn by default, to say what keeps us safe. When do we learn to take full responsibility for what comes out of our mouth? When do we realise the power we have on the tip of our tongue?

We, and what we say/don't say/withhold/listen to/believe/do/don't do, give us everything in our lives, and in our world. Everything began with a thought, an idea, in someone's imagination, that was expressed, then acted on, to cause a result. Are you willing to use your free speech to cause great results, even miracles, in the world? Are you willing to listen to what another has to contribute?

Was the end of slavery a 'miracle'? Would it have happened if people had not spoken so powerfully and passionately for its abolition, as a fundamental human right to freedom? What if it had not fallen on listening ears?

Would JFK have put a man on the moon if he had not said it so committedly? What if those listening had passed it off as fanciful nonsense? We may look but not see. We may see without looking. We can hear without listening and we can listen without hearing.

What is the truth? There's no 'truth' out there. There's what is true for me, and there's what is true for you. If I say I'm going to do something, and then I do that, I spoke the truth. If I said I was going to do something, and I didn't, I lied. If I say I'm going to do something and I continue to say it, knowing I'll do it, then it's the truth for me. If I say I'm going to do something and I continue to say it, knowing I'll not do it, then it's a lie for me.

Truth is fundamentally a personal matter. What is true for me may not be true for you. We must each discover for ourselves what level of truth we wish to live with. We're known by what we say. What we say about ourselves becomes what or who we are for others. When we're not true to ourselves, we're not true to others. We sometimes know when we're lying, but mostly it's hidden from our view. We've lied to ourselves for so long, we believe it to be the truth. Eventually, because we cannot live with ourselves as liars for too long, either the lie will kill us (maybe even literally!) or the truth will set us free.

But that takes courage. First, the courage to face ourselves and ask: am I lying to myself? Am I so far into my lie I no longer know where the truth ends, and the lie begins? Am I so deeply anaesthetised by the lie, I can't hear the truth? Where is the line between truth and lie? Who is the truth teller and who is the liar? We may prefer to die than face what we fear is the truth about ourselves, to have that truth be known. And what is that truth? For me it was that there was an unforgiveable, unlovable monster lurking somewhere in the deep recesses of my brain, running my life? A monster (a figment of my young imagination) who broke the doll, and reminded me that I was unlovable, unwanted, broken and unworthy. If this is the case for you, and you have a subconscious 'monster' running the show, perhaps it's time to 'wake up' and look under the bed. If you're scared, then fake it till you make it'. This may be more authentic than you think! At least you're practising to be who you want to be.

Who do you say you are? Is that the truth for you? Who is stopping you?

It takes courage to speak your truth

We can be trapped by what we say (and clobbered).

We can be liberated by what we say (and clobbered)

Either way, we can be 'clobbered' – meaning it can all go horribly wrong.

We can choose. Please them and stay silent, say nothing, stay safe, please our identity, our ego, our persona, while our 'self' suffers: our 'true self', the one we're here to express and be true to ourselves through self-expression and the truth of who we are. Should we risk it?

What is the alternative?

Self-expression is essential to life, otherwise we're merely surviving life. Without it, we become numb, strangers to ourselves, resigned and depressed. As we face the reality that we can't actually survive life, and we fail to kill the pain, we may simply choose to end the unbearable suffering ourselves. This is the ultimate tragedy. Our self-expression is our own responsibility – there's no one else coming. We hold the key!

Why are we here? To survive life, or to live life, to endure life or to enjoy life. We need to expand our horizons as to what's possible. We need to expand our consciousness, to become conscious of our own power, our power to master ourselves and our environment, to rise above victimhood, to escape the trap of what keeps us chained. We must learn to think as thinking human beings and embrace the opportunity of being fully human with all of our capacities. We are born to enjoy this wonderful experience of life on earth. Simply by virtue of being here we are gifted the beauty of this Garden of Eden, to enjoy its abundance, and share it with those we love.

How come we don't do that? What is it about the human condition that makes suffering so acceptable and happiness so elusive, when we're the source of all of it? Is there more to be gained by suffering? Are we letting ourselves off the hook for creating our own happiness?

We need to adjust ourselves. There are a lot of us here, and there's a lot to be done. Are harmony and cooperation so difficult? Are conflict and discord so easy? We use our most powerful tools to abuse – to abuse ourselves, to abuse others, to abuse our earthly home. We should be safe in our homes, in our relationships, safe in Mother Earth but we're like squabbling siblings fighting over toys. What is our resistance to sharing?

There is no planet B. There is no other time than now to get it right. There's no other place than here. There's no one else coming. We have everything we need. Whatever needs to be done, we must do it ourselves. Whatever needs to be said, we must say it ourselves. We cannot keep handing responsibility to the next generation of children, then thwart them with our own cynical fears that we too readily pass on.

We are born into a world of fear. Fear for our survival. That's the human condition. In primitive society this fear was justified. This fear is no longer necessary. We can master it. Most of us are not living in fear for our lives. We just need to admit that as human beings, we cannot escape the fear we are born with. We live in the fear of dying. What about the love of living? And courage? And trust? Could these be created such that we could live in a peaceful world? What then would we need to fear?

What are we afraid of? Ourselves? Other people? What else is there? What aspect of ourselves do we fear? Marianne Williamson wrote: "It is our light, not our darkness, that most frightens us."

We seem more familiar and comfortable with the 'darkness' – it lets us hide, protected and safe. But here, there are 'monsters' lurking – more fears- dangerous creatures feeding us those negative thoughts and beliefs that are so detrimental to our well-being.

How we're plagued by such thoughts. The demons in our minds. Take them out, look at them, shine the light on them, watch them disappear. They are the smokescreen, put there by a careless word or word of warning – a story before bedtime.

We listen and we learn

What are we teaching our children? What are we saying that they are hearing? What are we not saying that they are imagining? What are they learning?

We need to look at the results. We need to stop and look around and notice what is happening in the world. Really! And we need to say "we did this", not "they did that", because there is no 'they' out there.

Every time we point a finger, there are three more pointing back at us.

We need to stop and take stock, stop our frantic busy-ness and our doing, doing, doing, chasing, running around, in the rat race, and ask ourselves: what is it all for? A better life in the future? A better world? More money? More free time? To do what? When? In the future? What about now? What if now was all we had?

Some of us are pretending it's all great. We put on a good show for our neighbours, while gossiping and judging them behind their backs. We hope it will all work out. We worry that it won't. We wish for it to be some other way. We dismiss others' views in favour of our own. We blame others for what's not great in our lives. We complain that the world is not making us happy. We assume we have all the time in the world.

What is the cost of this pretence – to our health, sanity, relationships, communities, society, planet, our world? What if we admitted the truth- that we don't have it all handled – that we're 'winging' it as best we can – and that we're afraid to ask for what we need.

What a wonderful world it would be if more of us were able to accept what is real about our lives and acknowledge our role in causing it, the good the bad and the ugly. Taking action to correct what's not working so well. Picturing a desired future and taking the necessary steps to get there. Sharing our vision with others who will lead the way. Risking what we think we know for what we could discover. Listening to who is actually speaking and hearing what they are actually saying. Inspiring others to courageously step out from the shadows and shine their light in the world. Encouraging others to take the step and follow their own heart. Learning as we go; letting life teach us what we need to learn. Promising we will be true to our values, to do the best we can, where we are, with what we've got.

Look around – it's chaos. The chaos is expanding exponentially– on CNN and Twitter – and it multiplies like a virus. The world is infected with mean and hurtful words and they destroy as fast as they create mischief. Words create worlds. Words producing actions that result in something real and tangible in the world. We're extraordinarily powerful. We need to be accountable for how we use this power. We need to mind what we say.

We're the utterers of all the words: we are all speakers, writers, authors, broadcasters, elaborators, interpreters, translators, and influencers. With social media our words spread through society at an unprecedented rate – into the minds of people worlds away. Words are contagious and we are source of the 'contagion'. But we aren't behaving as if we're responsible, collectively, for that power. Do we know where our words go?

We seem surprised when someone listens: "Oh, but I didn't mean THAT..."

We could all contribute to the greater good, but instead, we share divisive opinions that make us sound clever, our individual concerns interfering with our capacity to cause real change, to impact those big conversations for harmony, justice, tolerance, inclusion, growth, prosperity and peace.

Until we are willing to be responsible for how we abuse our own power, out of fear and a desire to dominate, we will not be able to collectively deal with the major challenges that we face on a global scale. Yes, we have personal issues to deal with, however the same trust and courage that benefit one will benefit all. A rising tide raises all boats.

Look at the state of the world

Almost eight billion people. 8,000,000,000. Busy bees. Oblivious to the bigger picture. Only looking to the night sky for stars, those glimmers of light in the unfathomable enormity of the dark nothingness of the empty universe. We are so insignificantly small in the great scheme of things, yet seem blissfully unaware of our enormous potential.

The difference between bees and humans is that bees work together for a common purpose – the survival of the species. Human beings, however, are more interested in the survival of the individual identity – the 'me', the 'I', competing for scarce resources – food for me, money for me, land for me, love for me, attention for me, acknowledgement for me, appreciation for me, admiration for me. Like my survival depends on what you can do for me, not on what I can do for you, what we can do for each other, to ensure our survival, not realising that none of these resources are scarce, in the vast unharnessed potential of our personal universe. In fact, they are abundant, all within reach, and mostly within ourselves. It is our perception or illusion that they is scarce that makes them scarce, and so we fight over tiny morsels, trying to find them outside of ourselves, and kill each other over them. Madness.

As human beings, we're always striving for survival. We cannot survive life. From the moment we leave the safety of the womb, we're terrified we won't make it on our own. Until we can acknowledge and respect our source – our mother's love, and the love of Mother Earth – and realise the power of love is all we really need, we're doomed to wander the earth in search of it, not realising we're standing in it and we bring it with us everywhere we go. Connected to source, we have everything we need to live, and love, right here, right now. We just need to trust that and accept it. Happiness will follow.

This is the crux of my story. I found what I was looking for, exactly where I had left it.

An interview with myself

I often fantasised about being interviewed on TV – Oprah or Ellen or *The Late Late Show* – because I would have written a book that became a bestseller!

I'd be on the show speaking about my life, sharing my story with confidence and ease, and people would be listening, with attention, curiosity and interest, entertained, enlightened and inspired by my wisdom and insights. They would be encouraged and empowered in some way by my words and my contribution, realising that what was possible for me could be possible for many.

I'd be acknowledged for being the author of an influential book and I would have the experience of knowing what I had to say was indeed important and I would be proud and honoured to be seen and listened to as my natural, open, honest and authentic self, recognised for courageously trying to make the difference I wanted to make.

Then, I'd surely have made it: my life would be a success. I'd be fulfilled, happy and satisfied. I'd be leaving something important

206

after me – a book! A 'legacy'. My words would live on in people's minds: my words, spoken and written with the intention of being as a positive contribution to humanity. I'd be complete, ready to leave the world a better place for my having lived! And I could die happy!

Bliss.

But what would I be saying that was so important, that would justify me being there, being interviewed on TV? What could I possibly say that would've me become an author of a bestselling book? And how would I say it?

And what if it wasn't a bestseller? What if I'm never interviewed, never recognised and die never having been known? Will my life have been worthwhile? Will it have been significant? Will it have mattered that I existed?

Only if I say so!

What do you say about your life? I say my life is a journey of self-discovery and self-expression in a world where each of us has a place and a voice and a say in how our life goes. My intention is always to discover what is wanted and needed right now, who is listening and what they are listening for. Can I speak into that listening in a way that makes a difference for them?

What can I say that will connect, contribute, inspire, encourage, empower someone, somewhere, to live their best, one-and-only life, right here, right now?

What else do we have? Only our breath, and if our breath can carry a word of encouragement for another, it's a breath well spent. If I can breathe life into my words and commit them to paper, they've a good chance of falling into a listening ear and an open heart.

I started writing this book shortly before the death of my mother. What was so important that I had to say it?

I have no answers. All I ever had were questions. Did I really have something valuable to share?

I looked at my life. What could I do while I am here that might inspire another to live a bigger life, shine a brighter light?

Could I say that I had the courage to shine?

Would my attempt to overcome my fear of dying having never been known, as if I'd never been here, resonate with others? Is that fear there for others? I have no children. My siblings have their own lives. We share some memories, but for the most part we are relative strangers. Who could I trust to speak the truth about me? Who would know it?

And what could they say? Would it be kind? Would it even be vaguely true? Would it matter? In 500 years? What if it did?

All that truly matters is how we live while we're here. Life presents such unique opportunities that we so often waste. We do things we regret. We get to the end of our lives and wonder: what was it all for? Some believe the rewards will be in an afterlife, others believe they will come back and be given another chance to 'get it right'. Some say they've no belief in anything other than this life. Others, like me, want to believe in Heaven, but while doubt exists, we hedge our bets, try to do the right thing, and if there's a Heaven, we've a good chance of being 'let in'. We may still have memories from childhood, of stories or images, warnings of eternal damnation and burning in the fires of hell! It's a scary thought.

So, what have I discovered in the course of my life, on my journey, that could be told in the story of my life, that could be of value to you and worth the time taken to read it? Perhaps I've shared something that touches and inspires you and leaves you with a new possibility in your own life. I may have said something that shines a light in a hidden corner of your mind that miraculously lightens your load. You might have heard for yourself a new opening for taking action and caused a result in your life that wasn't going to happen otherwise.

What I do hope is that, in some small way, you will wake up to the wonder and opportunity of life, especially your life, and courageously face those fears that may be holding you back from living your best, biggest and brightest one-and-only life. You owe it to the world to shine brightly – we're all potential stars lighting the way for others. When we hide our light, others remain in darkness. When we refuse to shine, the world is deprived of our light, and the unique gift that we are for humanity remains unopened, undiscovered, unappreciated and unloved.

I spent my life saving lives, but no one noticed. I lived in the background, wore a mask, spent my days in pyjamas, put people to sleep. I watched over them. I kept them safe. I woke them up. The work of the anaesthetist exists in a dream world. No one sees what we do. The patient is unconscious. The surgeon is preoccupied. We're vigilant, trained to notice the smallest of changes, and intervene immediately. We're critically aware of what's happening, second by second. Life hangs in the balance, in our hands. Yet, we don't figure in the reality of most people. We're hidden and silent, in the background of the surgeon's heroic efforts to save lives: observing, watchful, anaesthetising so you don't have to be aware, so you don't feel pain, so you don't suffer. You are unaware of what we're doing, all the while we're doing it, being there, keeping you alive. We don't receive much in the way of acknowledgement, gifts or gratitude. When we're with you, you are asleep. You don't remember us. There's a mystery about us, an assumption that someone must be doing something, but you don't want to know. You just want to be unconscious for the duration and wake up when everything is done! You don't know how much you really depend on us; how much you trust us. Perhaps you don't want to know how vulnerable you are and what that responsibility is like for us? For that short time, your life is in our hands. For the remainder of your life, it's in your own.

I want you to wake up and become conscious of who you are, as your whole, healed self. You are in safe hands, safe in the universe. Trust you are in the perfect place and be grateful for the journey that you took to get here. Claim your voice and your power and shine brightly in this world. The world needs you.

CHAPTER 14

The Road to Happiness is an Inward Journey

*To forgive is to set a prisoner free and discover that the prisoner was you. – **Lewis B. Smedes***

It took me a long time to realise I loved my mother – really loved her. And to tell her. That was the point of no return. That was the moment I came home to myself, to the source of my one-and-only, beautiful life. And to thank her, for all of it, and forgive myself for taking my love away from her. To forgive her for 'making me' the monster child who broke the beautiful doll.

I was never the monster child who hated her mother. I was the scared child who thought her mother didn't love her enough to protect her. I was the nice, normal child who simply wanted to belong. I got trapped in being nice – and silent: trapped behind the glass pane, the invisible prison.

I hated it. I just wanted freedom – to be who I was meant to be – before the tablets!

When I heard my own words – the scales fell from my eyes, I realised how selfish I was for all those years, blaming her for how my life had turned out. When I looked at my life and saw what others saw, I saw what a great life I had. I knew I needed to thank her for everything, it had all turned out perfectly, not despite her, but because of her.

She was my mother, the source of it all. And I fell in love with her and loved her for that, like I'd just rediscovered what love was, and it was right there, where it had been all along. It was me who had been blind – and deafened by my own story.

For years we had fought. What is it they say about mothers and daughters? Too alike? But we were probably best friends – I had no sisters and Mam was always interested in what was going on in my life. We argued and disagreed, mostly about inconsequential things: my hair, clothes, boyfriends, but not with any real passion.

I was clearly a disappointment to her growing up as her only daughter, with no interest in clothes or shopping, probably deliberately to displease her. Why? Because I was angry with her, couldn't forgive her. Not realising it was myself I needed to forgive.

I regret that it took me so long. I could've had more fun shopping. She had lovely style – I could've learnt something. But I just had to find some subtle way to punish her.

I don't think she noticed. Neither the punishment nor the fact I was suffering. I didn't let on: just suffer in silence and punish at every opportunity, reject all her attempts to get close to me, hug or comfort me, to be my mother. I just pushed her away. It was all her fault, after all. I was her fault, after all.

Her fault? How crazy. I was her child, I was her 'gift'. I was her contribution to the world, and I am the difference she made. Without me, her life and legacy would be less.

And I have no children. What contribution will I make? As her daughter? Her legacy? I want my voice to be heard. I want the suffering to stop.

Mam's sister used to say she "can't die yet" because she has "not suffered enough". She died at ninety-four. That's what she believed. I believe that's a terrible lie. There's more to life than suffering. This is not 'our lot'! Our punishment for 'original sin'! I struggled to believe that, banished from the Garden of Eden, we are doomed to wander the earth; that we will be happy in Heaven – if we get in! – and until then, we're mourning and weeping in this valley of tears. This is what our young minds were taught. Why??

That's the crime of religion: while exhorting us to trust our higher self spiritually, we are threatened with punishment to tame our baser sinful instincts, perpetuating the myth that suffering, purgatory, and death are the only access to the promised land. The cycle is endless. What if we revisited these beliefs as adults? Surely love is simple? It is us who complicate it with doubt. We suffer when we fail to love or be loved, and we punish those who fail to love us.

We must start by loving ourselves. This sounds so obvious yet seems so elusive. What does it even mean?? For me it meant accepting the love of my mother, the source of my life. Without fully accepting my life and fully acknowledging, with profound gratitude, that my

213

mother was the source it, if I loved my life, then I loved my mother, who loved me, therefore I could love myself. Denying my mother would be denying myself. Resenting my mother would be resenting myself. Punishing my mother was punishing myself. Loving my mother was loving myself. How could I love myself if there was hatred in my heart?

Love is the source of it all. A mother's love is the source of her child's life.

We hear it every day – all religions preach it: love your neighbour as yourself. That's the rub – to love yourself, you have to love your mother/father, your source, no matter what they did. You are you because they are who they are, and they did what they did, or didn't do. Can we have compassion for all those mothers who didn't experience the love of their own mother, or child, the generational upset, the inability to express what was in their own hearts, for fear of judgement or shame? Motherhood comes with its own 'baggage' – its own 'sin of commission'.

Self-acceptance is the first critical step. Accepting all of you. And then accepting our parents. But mostly we want to blame and punish them, for all the mistakes they made, for not loving us enough, so how can that equate with self-love? Why do we do that? Why can we not see ourselves and love ourselves like our mothers did the moment they clapped eyes on us? Why can we not see the perfect creature that they saw? What do we say when something happens? What do we say about ourselves, about them? Why do we want to prove them wrong? "My teeth. My freckles. My nose. My stammer. It's all your fault."

She would say "speak properly" and I'd say "I CAN'T". Perhaps "I won't" would've been more honest in the beginning, but then I got trapped in the lie. And the lie had more power: it made it her fault. She just wanted me to be happy. I didn't want to give her what she wanted.

I had been surrounded by photos for months. I had gathered hundreds to put into a pictorial autobiography of my own life, and then compiled the smaller version for my aunt's ninetieth birthday three days before Mam died.

Mam passed away peacefully in her sleep, after eighty-nine happy years. Her work here was done. She saw her entire life in the pages of that book and was satisfied. Her life was complete. There was nothing left to do. She was free to leave. What a beautiful way to die. She simply slipped away and passed over. Thank you, God – her prayers were answered – a happy life and a peaceful death. And we both knew she was already in heaven.

I say she didn't go far. And she left something important after her. Me. And all the wise, loving words she spoke, that I can now hear.

I say we all pass into the next breath of someone who speaks our name. What they say on our passing depends on what they have in their hearts. It would be good to hear this when we are alive, to know we are loved. We get to choose the words we speak.

Martin Luther King said: "Our lives begin to end the day we become silent about things that matter." What if we get to say that our lives matter? What if I had died before I had a chance to write my story? This is my chance to be known by my own words. This is my opportunity to make my words matter.

Obituaries are rarely challenged. For those who lived in obscurity, and died with their secrets unknown, what lights were extinguished before they got the chance to shine? Who never wrote the truth about their lives? Did they live? Did their lives matter? What if everyone had the opportunity to be seen and heard as the shining lights they were born to be? What if life didn't send us into hiding, and leave us there, afraid, alone, in the dark? What if all around us were shining lights inviting more of us into the light?

Jewel was a shining light for me. In that swimming pool, in Bali, on a starlit night in 2013, Jewel's dark eyes twinkled as she uttered those magic words: "Write a book."

And with an "OK, I will", I accepted her challenge. If I truly wanted to be known for who I am, and what I say, and what I stand for, I would need to find the courage to write a book. When I started to write, the courage came.

So, who do you say you are, and what do you say your life is about? What do you stand for? What difference do you want your words to make?

Big questions, and my attempt to answer them is what appears on the pages of this book you now have in your hands. My life is in your hands. And remember, your life is in yours.

I'm an ordinary person who has a big dream. My dream world is a world devoid of unnecessary suffering and conflict: a world of peace, love and harmony. Peace in our mind and love in our heart. Simple.

I'm reminded of the story of the two wolves. A native American grandfather was talking to his grandson about how he felt. He

216

said: "I feel as if I've two wolves fighting in my heart. One wolf is the vengeful, angry, violent one. The other wolf is the loving, kind compassionate one."

The grandson asked him: "Which wolf will win the fight in your heart?"

The grandfather answered: "The one that I feed."

Some human beings spend a lot of time and energy feeding the vengeful wolf. How would the world look if there were no punishment, because there were no reason to punish? Would suffering stop? It seems obvious that when we stop punishing ourselves and others, we can stop suffering. Why do we punish others? To see them suffer? Why do we punish ourselves? To justify our suffering? Why do we suffer? In order to justify the punishment? Is this the eternal vicious circle? Can we interrupt it? Are we willing? Where do we start? When do we start?

Here and now would be a good time.

Because this is my dream, it requires that I share it, that my words and my voice be heard, and because I want this to happen sooner rather than later, my words need to reach as far and as wide as possible. This book is my message, and you are my messengers. Are you interested in a world without punishment? Are you interested in living life such that the threat of eternal suffering as punishment for our evil ways is removed from our consciousness? Are you interested in discovering that heaven really is here on earth and we don't need to wait for the afterlife to enjoy it?

The impact of this book does not need to manifest in my lifetime. There are generations waiting for us to get it right. It will not happen overnight. This is my attempt to create a dent in the universe. With your assistance, it can happen.

What would a dented universe look like? What if our planet wasn't suffering from the punishment we're meting out to it? What if we didn't rape and pillage our resources to feed our greed and punish all those who stood in our way? What if we shared what we had? What if another's happiness and self-expression were as critical as our own? There's an abundance of resources in the world. We will not live forever.

What if we were net givers, not net takers? What if we didn't suffer so saw no need to punish? I want to encourage and empower people to recognise and interrupt the suffering-punishment cycle, starting with being aware of our own. Suffering exists because we let it persist. We don't suffer in the here and now – not unless we're physically being tortured, or brutalised, or hurt. Most of our suffering exists because we recall something from the past, and relive it, over and over, retell it, re-experience it, redramatise it, recreate it, and so dwell in that world we've designed as a way of justifying some story we have about it. But it's not happening now, in the present; it only exists in the telling of it. And, as we tell it, over and over, we perpetuate it. Others listen and inherit the conversation as surely as if it were their DNA. The conversation keeps it alive and it feeds itself. Perhaps it's time to stop talking and start listening, for something new.

If we want to be happy, we must learn to forgive, and forget. We must learn to let go that which does not serve our happiness. Leo Tolstoy said: "If you want to be happy, be." If we want something new, we must be clear about what that is. The universe will give us exactly what we want. What exactly do you want? We cannot go back to the past to get what we wanted then. There's no future in the past and there's no past to go back to. All we ever have, and ever had, is the present moment.

Now is the perfect moment to reflect on that, to let go of any resentment or grudge or regret from the past and to choose what you truly want in your life right now. The present moment. What you do in this moment matters. This moment IS your life. This is it. You are here. You matter.

Now what? Reliving the past over and over keeps it alive – there's no new 'cheese' down that tunnel. If we want new cheese – we must look in a different direction. We must look forward and not back. We must look for what has not yet been. We must create it. We must visualise it in our mind's eye. We can do that with our word. We can say things we've never said, or that others have said. If we continue to say things that we've always said, we are unlikely to hear something new. Things that got us here may not take us where we want to go. We can all be like Martin Luther King or Gandhi or JFK; courageous people who shared their dreams, who said something new and radical, that caused old conversations to disappear. India was liberated peacefully. A man walked on the moon. Slavery was abolished. Women got to vote. The earth is no longer flat. Or that human beings are not born to suffer in this life!

I've spent much of my life trying to get to the core of 'who I am' and how did "I", the person people call Eileen Forrestal, come to be the person I AM, that I know myself as, or that others know me as. If you ask them, that's unlikely to be anything like the person I know myself as, or how my mother knows me, or my best friend, neighbour, colleague or a stranger on a plane. So, from that, I know I'm not one person, but that I occur differently to different people – I'm not a fixed entity, carved in stone. I also know that, on any given day, I'm not even the same person. I can blow hot and cold, happy and sad, upset and funny, irritated and compassionate, mean and kind, selfish and generous, kind and nasty. It goes on. I respond and react to my environment, to who is there and to what is going on around me and what is going on inside me! I show up differently in different places and with different people, at different times. I'm the sum total of all I've ever heard, experienced, witnessed, embodied – and by this time tomorrow, I'll have added more to myself. I'm multifaceted, and multi-faced with multiple capacities to respond in multiple ways. I'm a human being: a miracle, mysterious, amazing, terrifying! I'm in awe of myself, and yet I'm an ordinary human being, no different from you. And I'm in awe of you.

And, yes, I suffered. And, yes, I punished. However, I got to the source of it, and let it go. And, yes, I may continue to suffer, and I may continue to punish; I'm human. But now I know I've a choice. Now I choose not to suffer and not to punish.

What is my message?

To be clear at the outset, I have no desire for fame or celebrity or any significant wealth or notoriety. It's not about me, Eileen Forrestal; it's about my message, and what I say my life is about. I'm just a messenger and my life is my message.

We all know the romance of the message in a bottle – a few words written on a page, sealed in a bottle and tossed into the ocean, to turn up on some foreign shore, in some future time, with some message from the past. The mystery: what does it mean and who sent it?

Well, this is me – my message in a book. I've shared my story and you can decide what it means for you – from now when I'm writing it – to some future now when you are reading it. In the meantime, the world will have changed for both of us. Nothing stays the same.

People have asked me: "What IS your message?" My life is my message, as your life is your message – how does one express a life in one sentence? It's taken me a whole book, and I'm still discovering it. Perhaps in the reading of my writing, you will hear words that are relevant for you. Certainly, in writing it, I discovered new relevance in reading many of my own words. Perhaps there will be one sentence that will resonate with you, that you will take away as your message. Like in a bookstore, or a supermarket, when we were sent out for errands (or messages) as children – we all came home with what we needed, and maybe even some change. And if we didn't get what we wanted, we could always go back. There are lots of words here, in lots of sentences – it may just take one to change your life. And perhaps enough changed lives can change the world.

With the internet and social media, the explosion of voices and messages, we all have an opportunity for our voices to be heard. Now it's a cacophony – but who is listening? What messages are we now getting from these disembodied voices hidden behind screens? What is true? What is real? What is fake? What can be trusted? Is the message getting lost in the noise and confusion of it all? Are we getting lost? Are we all trying to communicate the same thing? Do you see me? Do you love me?

Social media is still a medium – a between space, between me and you. It's a medium designed to connect us but it's actually separating. We're in danger of becoming so disconnected from who we are, from the person we are, that we disconnect from 'reality' and suffer the breakdown of our psyche.

We need community. We need connection. We need to deal with our existential loneliness together. That is what we're here for. That is what gives meaning to our lives: the simple fact we contribute to one another.

As we get further lost behind the screens – observing, and showing, an idealised yet unreal world, we're now actors and directors in plays of our own scripting, to get widespread approval. We become blind to who we and others really are. We are learning to distrust this 'veil' between them and us: the medium, the smokescreen, the mask, the layer we show, the veil of secrecy, the 'fake news", the 'screen' we can hide behind. But now, who do we trust? Do we trust ourselves to show ourselves? What is so threatening about being seen? Are we like the electrons under the microscope such that, in the split second of being seen, and being recognised as an electron, they jump? Do we jump as soon as we're seen – back into the safety of the (dark) web?

There are plenty who choose to stay hidden, spreading poison like a virus, infecting everything, with negativity, with fear, with toxic bullying. More punishment, leading to more suffering that spirals exponentially. Those of us with something else to say need to say it. We must not be stopped by fear.

"The only thing necessary for the triumph of evil is for good men to do nothing." Edmund Burke

None of us can look away and say it has nothing to do with us. This is our world. These are our brothers and sisters, our fellow human beings, and they are suffering and punishing.

So, I decided to write the book and trust that you who have picked it up will read it for yourself, and that my message will communicate to you, because you are listening. That is your gift to me, your listening, and for that I thank you. I appreciate you, and I'm happy to share my life with you.

I hope you can see that I'm not at all different from you, and the journey I'm on, from the cradle to the grave, is not dissimilar. Perhaps it may look like I'm on a different path or further down a different road or even behind. I ask you to be patient and sit with me a while. Wherever you are in your life, I'm here too. Life is happening now, so we're all here, now: no one is ahead or behind. We're all exactly where we are, and where we are meant to be. I know that fundamentally you and I are ordinary human beings doing our best with what we have on this journey through life. We can look back, look around, look forward, but essentially, we're here, now, living and breathing and feeling and thinking and experiencing life as it's happening.

I can look back on my life as you can look back on yours and we can each reflect on the choices we made that got us here. I can look forward to a future where I know I'll be presented with more choices that will be different from yours. What unites us, however, is our humanity: we each have a purpose, unique value, gifts and talents, strengths and weaknesses, an opportunity to show up in the twenty-first century, wherever we are, to shine our light, contribute to the greater good, and the power to choose where, when, how and why.

We exist in a vast outer universe and are careering through space at an incredible, yet imperceptible speed. We also exist in an inner universe, equally as vast and fathomless, and often that has us feeling as if internally we're also spinning out of control. We live on a planet with its relentless seasons and changing weather. We live in a country with a population of different ages and genders, all going about their day-to-day lives within different boundaries and religions, historical narratives and cultures. What keeps us grounded? Our senses. Our sight, smell, touch, hearing and taste. We just need to open our eyes and ears and connect authentically with another human being or living creature and we can get present to who and where we are. We don't even need to speak. In fact, it's what we say that often separates us, disconnects us, through misunderstanding or confusion and, worse, through lies and falsehoods.

One thing we can trust, however, is that our bodies will function to keep us alive, for as long as we take care of them, or for as long as they're needed for us to get our work done here.

We arrive on this earth delivered in an incomplete state: innocent, dependent, small, defenceless, fearful and trusting. We do our best to fit in and learn how to survive and function within our society, with its norms and rules and expectations. We're born into a family with its own history and inherited conversations and norms and rules and expectations. We arrive with a seemingly blank canvas – but with a pre-written charter. We've already inherited the 'constraints' of our human limitations – we may even inherit societal limitations, or gender or class, but we're possibly most gifted (or cursed) with a mind of unlimited imagination and potential, constrained in a human body – an earthling form with its limited physical abilities and yet its own vast inner universe.

How do we reconcile these attributes? How does our 'self' get expressed given the limits of our personal identity? What happens to those thousands of ways of being that are available to us when we become fixed in some way by the listening (speaking) of others? "He's stupid" "He's useless" Or, worse, in the speaking (listening) of ourselves: "I'm stupid," "I'm no good at that," "I'm a waste of space." Trapped mercilessly in the momentary utterance of someone's ignorant or careless words, we take on the label like a blanket of truth. What if we could bask freely in the fresh air of silent acceptance, rather than desperately trying to avoid drowning in the sea of judgement?

It's no wonder we find ourselves scrambling to make sense of the incomprehensibility of everything, including ourselves, and find ourselves lost and alone. We use language to try to find meaning in what others say and do, and to try to understand and make sense of the world and each other, just seeing the superficial, all the while oblivious to another's internal universe, as unfathomable as our own. We struggle to make sense of it all. We try to control the uncontrollable – other people – and therefore suffer in our relationships, in our families, workplaces, communities and ultimately in ourselves. We wonder why we break down in tears of frustration, failure and despair, overwhelmed by our self-inflicted compulsion to try to figure it all out, so we can 'know' all of it, understand all of it, and ultimately understand ourselves.

Who can know and understand all of it? Why do we so desperately need to know everything? So we won't appear lacking, foolish or stupid? So we won't be caught out? I discovered this compulsion for myself – my six-year-old self was desperate not to be caught out as so 'stupid' ever again! That was an exhausting life sentence for a curious child.

Unfortunately, most of us are still looking out instead of looking in. The answers to the questions we seek aren't out there. As our outer world expands, we can find ourselves drowning in information overload and losing sight of the bigger picture (our humanity) and the smaller picture (ourselves) within it. We give ourselves an impossible task and fail miserably. In despair and exhaustion, we resign ourselves to our fate: death is coming to relieve us. In doing so, we put a lid on the coffin of our experience of being alive. We're too tired to shine our light. Our light is now extinguished in the sea of cynicism and resignation – that it's all pointless, too much, we're too small and weak and insignificant, and only fools believe in miracles. We stop swimming and float, hoping the current will take us gently to the shore.

What we think we learn from the past, that will help us avoid hurt in the future, doesn't always work in our favour. Our attempts to control the world, to make is safer, from what we think we know, often have unintended consequences. We think we need to know the danger up ahead to survive it, but by the time we're prepared to meet it, that danger has passed, and another danger has presented itself to us, from the blindside, that we weren't expecting. Now it seems we have to prepare for the expected and the unexpected, the probable and the improbable, the possible and the unpredictable and the unforeseen. All of a sudden, our life is over, and we've spent our lives preparing for what never happened and missed what was happening as it was happening. We're so busy preparing for winter, we miss the beauty of autumn. We're so busy preparing our children for a future we think (fear) is going to happen, we miss their presence in the present. We're so busy working hard, preparing to be successful and happy, we miss those beautiful precious moments with the people in our lives as they are happening.

What if we could choose to be in the wonder of it all as it unfolds and enjoy the journey of discovery? We could embrace the uncertainty of the 'unknown' and trust ourselves to bring forth a new order from the chaos, as we've always done, but from the truth of ourselves.

What if it were OK to simply be here now? To be present, grateful, happy, loving, forgiving, accepting, peaceful, proud? To be any of a million ways that human beings can be, such that those around us can experience being OK to simply be here now too? Nothing to do, nowhere to get to, just present to the miracle and opportunity of being human and being alive, right now, being related, and noticing where we can contribute, shine our light, make the world just that little bit better? Would that be a different world – and a different experience of being alive?

My role as author of this book is similar to my role as author in my life. The living of my life has bestowed on me an authority on myself. The writing of it allows me to reflect, interpret, make sense of my story, and to share it. I hope it will resonate somewhat with you, such that you get an opportunity to reflect on your own experience. Perhaps you'll discover how your life can be enriched because of it, because I shared my story, and had the courage to shine a light into some dark corners, the illuminating of which might light a way forward for you.

"The unexamined life is not worth living," according to Socrates. I believe it behoves us all to examine our lives, to discover for ourselves what makes us tick. Becoming an author is one way to discover who we are.

So much of my understanding of my life fell into place in the process of my writing it.

Chapter 15

89 Important Things I Want to Say

*"Our lives begin to end the day we become silent about
things that matter," – **Martin Luther King Jnr.***

Why 89? One for every year of my precious mum's life.

1. Thank you. For all of it. Without you there would be no me.
THANK YOU for being my mother, for choosing a career in nursing,
for coming to Dublin, choosing my father, carrying me, having me,
looking after me, always being there, for your unconditional love.
And thank you for being the person that had me say 'yes' in life.

2. I love you. That wasn't always an easy thing for me to say.

3. It was me who did it – I took the tablets. I thought it was clever of
me to find them, to share them between Brian and me. I thought it
was lucky when Brian didn't want his share and I could have all of
them. It was me who caused all the upset when you had to rush me to
hospital to have my stomach pumped. It was me who screamed stop,

that tried to tell you I was scared and they were hurting me. It was me who didn't understand why you were upset. I know now it wasn't because I was so bold for taking the tablets, but that you had lost your new baby, my baby brother, and I thought it was my fault. I didn't understand. It was me who tried to apologise and console you. It was me who got it wrong and thought it was all about me. It was me who thought that by me being a really good girl I would not upset you ever again. It was me who wanted to believe you when you told me I was going on my holidays when I was having my tonsils out. It was me who got really angry when I awoke with that terrifying pain in my throat. It was me who decided that I couldn't trust people who said they loved me. It was me who took my love away from you. It was me who punished you for what you did. It was me who suffered. It was me wouldn't forgive you for what I thought you had done. It was me who made you suffer. I needed to forgive myself, not you. Why should I forgive you for loving me??

4. Please forgive me. I was angry, upset and hurt. I was young. I was stubborn. I was unwilling to give in to you. I was determined you wouldn't 'get' me. I wanted to punish you. I'm sorry.

5. I'm sorry I did that. I'm sorry it took me so long to figure out how my impulsive decision not to trust anyone who said they loved me, played out in my life.

6. I didn't know that for a long time. I thought I was being clever.

7. I love how wise we both became in those last few years.

8. I'm grateful for the opportunity to get to know you as we both grew older.

9. I regret my immaturity and stubbornness that didn't let me see you as a person, on my side, not simply a mother, when we were both younger. We could've been better friends, going to the cinema, or shopping – I know you loved your style. You really were beautiful. I always thought you were very stylish – I just resisted your style, trying to assert my own. The trips to Rome, and Paris and Vienna were so wonderful. Even in your eighties you were the best travelling companion!!

10. I wish I'd known you as a young girl, as the dignified, stylish woman in the photographs, a real person, and known your hopes, dreams and fears.

11. I want other people to see the person in everyone, not simply the 'role' they play in each other's lives – mother, father, brother, sister, employer, employee, voter, patient, doctor, nurse, teacher. I want them to not simply see the character they play in our soap opera. You had that gift.

12. I know stuff about myself now; stuff you always knew. There's no hiding from our mother. I know why you loved me.

13. I don't know what the future holds beyond that which I design for myself, but you are guiding me from wherever you are.

14. I dream of being someone that others listen to and learn from, such that their lives are light and easy and peaceful and free. Everyone deserves to smile like you did.

15. I pray that humanity will see the light soon. We burden ourselves unnecessarily. We suffer needlessly. We punish without cause. We choose the comfort of the dark as we fear the exposure of the light.

16. The most important lesson I learnt is that it's never too late – for anything. The time is always just right, right now. And it's always now.

17. The saddest moments for me were losing you both, and seeing your grief when Dad died. Your disappointment that you couldn't mend the rift between my brother and me. How sad you were when you thought I'd be lonely without children of my own. When I failed to be happy – refusing to let myself be who you knew I was.

18. My happiest moments were when I was completely free, simply being myself, by myself, like when I was in the Alps, one afternoon, alone, in the Swiss Alps, singing my heart out, like Julie Andrews in *The Sound of Music*. I never told you about that. I knew you would have worried. There was no one to fear, and no one to hear me, so I sang at the top of my voice. Does that sound strange? We had some great laughs too, you and I. Remember the Moulin Rouge??

19. My proudest moments were when I overcame my greatest personal fear – speaking in public. I had many proud moments during my medical career when those I touched were better for it. I'm proud of my courage to take on jumping out of an airplane at 15,000 ft; crossing those fifteen terrifyingly rickety swaying wooden bridges high up in the Himalayan gorges; my abandon at being catapulted out of the Incredible Hulk at Islands of Adventure at Disney World in Florida; my generosity, and that so many people have thanked me for encouraging them to do something or, because of me, they found the courage to do something they had always wanted to. I know your proudest moments were when I qualified as a doctor, and got a job in the Mater, and later when I was awarded my Fellowship in Anaesthesia. I think Dad's proudest moment was walking me down the aisle when I got married. I'm sort of glad he wasn't around to see

me get divorced. He was very proud when I passed my driving test (after all his lessons) and when I told him I had bought my first home.

20. I forgive myself for keeping silent for so long. I forgive everyone for everything. Forgiveness is a gift we give ourselves. We must all live with the consequences of our own actions and omissions. We're all accountable for our actions. The crime can be forgiven but the criminal must pay some price. What is the price for a crime? We seem to think that 'jail' is the ultimate price to pay: our loss of freedom. We're kept away from regular people, excluded from society, shunned by the community. But for many criminals and prisoners, this may not be the ultimate punishment. Perhaps this has already been their experience of their own existence; maybe they already regard themselves as different, excluded, shunned. Perhaps they've no concept of freedom, having already been trapped in some horror in their own lives, knowing no way out, acting out their anger and frustrations. I don't know. I'm my own kind of criminal. It took me a long time to discover my crime, let alone confess. Had I been born to different circumstances, met different people, had different influences, different experiences, different responses, I might be a different kind of criminal. I stole blackcurrants once. They were from Mr Gibney's garden, remember? It was a dare. He was a policeman! I wanted to join the boy scouts. I thought I'd be caught and arrested and spend my life in jail. I'd seen jail on TV. It was dark and frightening. I knew I had to tell my sin in confession. And even if I could get the words out in my confession, the priest would know and he would have to tell the police and I would definitely be arrested and go to jail (I didn't realise at the time that confessional was confidential). I suffered in silence about this for a long time. I think that's the reason I never became a 'real' criminal. I didn't have the stomach for it. Sometimes we suffer in our own minds significantly worse than we might suffer in any jail. And the sentence is forever, or at least until

we set ourselves free. And we're the judge, jury, sentencer and the prisoner. The sentence is that we get to suffer in silence. How bizarre.

21. I accept that we are all on our own journey through this life. We share certain things, like space, time, air, water, words, ideas. I was lucky I got to share so much of my journey with you.

22. I love you. It's so easy to say it now.

23 I believe peace is possible. If we have peace in our own hearts and in our own minds, then we will have peace in the world. I believe we can have anything we want. If we want peace, all we need is to be is peaceful. There isn't much to do. I hear of people fighting for peace. That doesn't make sense to me. We can stand for it, speak about it, be it, but we can't make others peaceful. We can't even want peace – wanting it just keeps it further away. We already have it, in our heart. It's the mind that is restless.

24. I don't really believe in evil. I believe people are capable of doing evil things. I don't think anyone is born evil – babies are too beautiful to be evil. All babies are lovable and loving. I've met too many good people to believe in evil. What turns a good person into an evil person? Do good people resort to evil behaviour because of some distorted thinking? Do people seem evil simply because we don't understand them?

25. I understand the power of fear. Not in its true power, but certainly in its ability to control. Love is empowering. Love is the greatest power on earth. Fear engenders more fear. Love should create more love: love and fear in a constant dance. I believe in fear. Fear is the source, and outcome, of many evil acts. Do we fear evil? Of course we do. Sometimes we fear that perhaps we're capable of evil, and that

frightens us. I was sometimes cruel to the cat. I was upset and I took it out on the cat. I wasn't a bad person. I was sorry afterwards. I could've grown up to be a cruel person, but I didn't. Quite the opposite. I felt really sorry for the cat. I loved her. People do strange things, and don't even understand themselves why they do them. I think when we're disconnected from love, we can be cruel, we punish, and do things that can be seen as evil. And the more disconnected we are from ourselves and love, and any source of love, the more we punish ourselves and others. It's the cycle of suffering and punishment. The more we suffer, the more we punish.

26. I understand that, as a human being, I'm capable of doing many things, good and bad, right and wrong. Thank you for showing me how to be a good human being. All 'inhuman' acts we hear about in history, have all been perpetrated by human beings, not by aliens or strange fictional monsters. I don't really understand human nature. I barely understand myself, but I understand a lot more now than when I was younger.

27. I'm guilty of thinking I know better. This is not such a good thing.

28. I'm still excited by too many things. I love this about myself.

29. I aspire to inspire before I expire.

30. I have lots of great role models – besides you and Dad. Thanks to your example, I am drawn to people who represent the highest values of human beings: those who show courage, compassion, kindness and integrity, a desire to make a positive contribution in the world, who speak of peace and freedom and justice, who work to relieve pain, fear, hunger and suffering, who enjoy life and music and art and poetry and whose fun is never at someone else's expense. I honour

you both, and both my grandmas and the granddads and all the great grandmothers and great grandfathers I never met. I'm standing on the shoulders of giants.

31. My hopes are for good health, peace of mind and happiness for my family and friends and the family and friends of everyone I know and love. My wishes are for peace and reconciliation between those of us who are separated by history or misunderstanding. My dreams are for all who are lost to find the courage to discover who they truly are, and to love who they find in the process. I like to expect miracles.

32. My plans are many and always changing. I keep a diary, or three...

33. My intentions are almost always good. My intention is always to contribute – positively. The outcome is not always as I intend. I'm often misunderstood, frustrated and upset when my intentions to be a contribution are thwarted or unwanted. Sometimes I irritate people with my enthusiasm. Sometimes I can be overpowering and forceful.

34. My commitment is to do good in the world, to not intentionally upset anyone, to help and support where I can, and to push the boundaries of what is possible for me through ongoing exploration of who I am and what drives me, through personal growth and development. I've always known that life is exciting outside the comfort zone – and it seems like I've been outside my comfort zone for most of my life. It's just that I'm now further out – waaaay further out – and loving it!

35. My voice is my access to everything. But other people's listening gives me my self-expression. I don't hold back now. I could speak for Ireland! My words flow like a mighty river whether I'm speaking or

writing, when I give voice to my thoughts. I take every opportunity to be heard, to be listened to, to contribute. This is the greatest gift of all.

36. What's important to me is that my life is used for something purposeful, notable, noble, memorable, that my being here made a difference to someone. I know it made a difference to you.

37. What I care about is that we all care about each other.

38. My country is in my DNA. I'm an Irish woman. My country is Ireland. I'm of Ireland. I love my country, its people, history, geography, everything that makes it what it is, my home and my nation. Its people fought for me. Its people died for my freedom. Its people stood for my peace. It is part of who I am. Without Ireland, I would be someone else. I love who I am. I love being Irish. I love my country, my motherland; Mise Eire is in my bones.

39. My education has been one of my greatest gifts. It has given me access to the most wonderful opportunities. My health has been another. I'm blessed with the most valuable of gifts. I'm truly a wealthy woman.

40. The person I am is because of the person you are.

41. Thank you for being the mother who had me say "yes" in life.

42. I loved it when you said I had become the person you hoped I would be when I was three. I'm sorry for making you wait so long.

43. I had a great time.

44. Thank you for all your prayers.

45. Everything is "all right", just like you said it would be.

46. I still have work to do – my job is not done yet.

47. Did I ever tell you that you were truly the best Mum in the whole world? Did you believe it? Do you believe it now? It's the truth.

48. I'm happy. You did a great job. I brought any misery on myself. You were always there to pick up the pieces and mend my broken heart. My heart is mended. You can rest in peace. Thank you for creating a home I could always come home to. Home is truly where the heart is.

49. Say "Hi" to Dad for me. Oh, he's there ... put him on and I'll talk to him myself.

50. Hi Dad. I know you are proud of me now. I know you always were. I just wasn't too proud of myself.

51. I promise I will honour you always.

52. You did a great job. It was hard for you as you didn't have a father of your own to guide you. But you took on two perfect role models – The Sacred Heart and St Francis of Assisi.

53. There was a reason you didn't die when you got sick...

54. Blessed are the peacemakers.

55. Thank you for teaching me the Prayer of St Francis of Assisi:
"Lord, Let me be an instrument of your peace;
where there is hatred, let me sow love;

where there is injury, pardon;
where there is doubt, faith;
where there is darkness, light;
where there is sadness, joy.
Grant that I may not so much seek
to be consoled, as to console;
to be understood, as to understand;
to be loved, as to love;
for it's in giving that we receive,
it is in pardoning that we're pardoned,
it is in dying that we're born to eternal life."

56. I remember the story of the Cherokee Indian and his grandson: it's the wolf you feed that wins.

57. Thanks for all the holidays.

58. And helping me with my Maths homework.

59. And not giving me too much pocket money.

60. And not stopping me from going to medical school.

61. And helping me buy my first house.

62. And teaching me to drive.

63. And not slapping me when it was what I deserved!!

64. And for loving our country.

65. And for the hours of political debate.

66. And for letting me watch *The Late Late Show*.

67. And for patiently explaining what I didn't understand.

68. And for filling in all those forms.

69. And for harassing my boyfriends – no one was ever going to be good enough for me (I forgive you – it's a tough job finding someone to come up to your standards and ideals).

70. For getting better when you were so sick and giving me enough time to get to know you and acknowledge you.

71. For giving up smoking, after fifty-five years. I know how difficult that was for you.

72. For living with one lung.

73. And hanging in there.

74. Until you could get home and die in your own bed.

75. For always being "just in the other room".

76. For all the lifts and taxi runs.

77. For the picnics ... and the camping trips...

78. For listening.

79. For caring.

80. For loving Mam.

81. For loving all of us

82. For being:

83. Kind.

84. Good-humoured.

85. Dependable.

86. Safe.

87. A loving,

88. Lovely man.

89. Thank you for being my father. I love you, Dad.

Conclusion

"I know why the caged bird sings" – **Maya Angelou**

Mam died. She went to sleep and didn't wake up. Exactly like she prayed for.

At least that's what they said happened. I've been thinking about that. How does one die in one's sleep? Does the heart just stop, or did she get a pain or a fright like a nightmare, and wake up, and then die? How would we know?

The nurse said when she checked her at 1 a.m. she was sleeping, but when she checked at 1.30 a.m. she felt cold.

I think she died at 1.20 a.m., when the phone rang. I was writing. Then it stopped. I think Mam was saying goodbye.

I miss her now. I miss her being alive: somewhere, anywhere.

As I drove to the nursing home, alone, in the dead of night, to be with my dead mother, for one-and-a-half hours, what was I thinking? Of life and death and the inevitability of it all. What was my life about? What would she say if she were sitting in the car beside me?

"Don't cry. Everything will be all right."

All those years of tears: "Stop punishing me; I love you." And all my: "Stop hurting me; I'm suffering."

Death has a way of stopping things.

All we didn't do was Stop It!

In all the noise, no one heard: "I love you."

Mam has now passed on the living to me. Everything she was, is now me. It's up to me to carry on as her light in the world.

I want to live a big life. Until I found my own voice, my experience of my life was that I was small, that I was insignificant, that I made no real difference to anyone. That, of course, was not the truth. I was an experienced doctor, an accomplished anaesthetist. I had lots of letters after my name. I made a difference every day to someone's life. Some days I was the difference between life and death. It was an awesome responsibility, too awesome to contemplate some days, so most days I just did my job. I also believed that anyone could be trained to do what I did, I was not unique. I was good but not brilliant. I was interested but not passionate. However, my experience was that something was missing. I was missing.

There was another difference that I wanted to make. I wanted to make the world better, not just the 'patients' that I met. I wanted everyone to want to make the world better, and I wanted to help people to do that. I'm not sure I knew how to do that, not until now, not until I said it out loud, so others could hear it. I have an 'impossible promise' for the world. This is the umbrella under which I live my life – that covers and colours everything I do – from the moment I get up in the morning until I go to bed at night – that each and every person can know themselves as whole, perfect, complete and loved, present to the unique gift they are to humanity, and empowered to be at the source of their own health, wellbeing and happiness. I do not want people to be victims in their lives, like me, suffering in a drama of their own making.

I do not see myself as a 'saviour' of anyone. I had a career in 'saving lives'. People don't need to be saved. People need to be liberated from the prisons of their own thinking. I want people to realise the power they have in their own words to create the lives they want for themselves. People are immensely powerful. When people realise the power of their word, then they can change their world. The tongue is the most flexible muscle in the body. The pen is indeed mightier than the sword. No matter what you tell yourself, you are the source of your own experience of life and all that you say about it. Own your own interpretation. Own your voice. Your voice is you in the world. Discover the gift that you are and share yourself proudly with those you love. Let it light up your life and you will light up the world.

In discovering that you have spent your life hiding, you can now venture out from the shadows. You can only go forward from where you are, so you must identify where you are. Look around you, see where you are, and now decide what direction you want to go. You know you can't go back and create a new beginning, but you can start here and design a new ending.

There are some questions you need to ask yourself before you embark on this journey, the answers to which will give a glimpse of whether this 'daring adventure' will be a worthwhile venture for you.

Where are you right now, today, on your life's journey?

Do you recognise the choices you made that got you here?

Do you have a vision or a desire of how you want the future to be?

Are you willing to make the turn if it requires a change in direction?

Are you ready?

If not, when will you be ready?

If not, will the tomorrow you create today become a yesterday you regret?

If not, will there be more tomorrows spoiled, or thwarted, by fear, or anger or resentment?

If not, how many of tomorrow's dreams will be put off, for one more day, one more month, one more year, waiting until you are 'ready'?

I invite you to start at the start. Today, now, here.

You have heard it many times – that today is the first day of the rest of your life. And it really is. So, what do you want for the rest of your life? Say it now – and mean it. For there is only now, and it's happening now.

You are here today. You were somewhere yesterday. You may be somewhere else tomorrow. But you are here now. This is your point of power. Do you notice that today is the tomorrow you talked about/ worried about/ wondered about yesterday? Will today become a yesterday you regret tomorrow? Or will today be the day that alters the course of all your tomorrows?

Will you promise something today that ensures tomorrow will not be a day that was 'going to happen anyway'? Will you say yes to that invitation today? Will you register for that course today? Will you have your last cigarette today? Will you book that holiday today? Will you make that call, write that letter, apply for that job, start to write that book which changes your life today? How many todays are wasted, waiting for the 'right' time?

How many todays are spoiled by worrying about yesterday or tomorrow, and how many tomorrows are spoiled by an argument today? Are you willing to start having a life of well lived todays as you create the tomorrows of your dreams?

And it's that simple.

What comes out of your mouth, designs your life.

Acknowledge yourself for getting yourself here, everything you ever did was to get you to this precise point in your life, right now. How do I know this? Because otherwise you would be somewhere else, doing something else, and you would not be reading this book.

So, yes, you are here. You have arrived. This is where you got to. This is where you are on your journey through life. The baggage you have gathered along the way is all yours. Accept it. Love it. And, if it's heavy, and weighing you down, maybe, just maybe, it's time to let it go. The past is past. It's not coming back.

Avoid the pitfall of regret. It took everything to get you here. Life is unfolding perfectly. You are who you are. Do you like yourself? Sure you do. Sometimes! Do others like you? Sure they do. Sometimes! Have you ever done something you wish you hadn't done? Sure you have. Does it matter one jot right now? Is there anything that cannot be cleared up in a conversation? Forgive yourself. Forgive others. Move on. It's what you do now that matters. It's what you say now that matters. Take heed of the lessons in this book. Some of them were hard learned. Now go out and make the world a better place for having you in it – and make sure you have fun. That's the true test of a great life – you love living it – and the world can tell by your smile.

It's now my time to shine.

For me it's like smiling – from the inside.

It's also saying what needs to be said, without fear.

What is happening now in the world that should not be happening, and it is, and we are not doing or saying anything about it? Are people being subjected to cruel and humiliating treatment, are they suffering the pain of injustice, the stigma of shame, the loneliness of disconnection – and we stay silent? This can happen in our own homes, in our relationships with our nearest and dearest. This is where we need to start.

I can't stop the wars. I can't feed the hungry. I can't end the torture. I can't stop the crime. But I can stop hurting people. I can stop punishing people. I can stop hurting myself. I can stop punishing myself. I can stop suffering. I can stop using my words as weapons and start using them to repair broken relationships. I'm sorry. Please forgive me. I love you.

I can stop being afraid and be courageous.

I can stop worrying and be confident.

I can stop arguing and be peaceful.

All this suffering is so unnecessary,

We are all the same. We all just want to be loved.

So, stop doing what doesn't work.

STOP

Stop it!

Why?

It doesn't work.

Mother's logic.

"Little birds in their nest agree."

Letters from Heaven

Dear Eileen,
I know who you are.
I'm sorry if I hurt you.
Forgive me.
I love you.
Mam

Dear Mam,
You never hurt me.
I hurt myself.
I'm sorry I punished you.
Forgive me.
I'm happy.
I see you smiling in Heaven
I love you.
Thank you for my life.
Eileen

Dear Dad,
Thanks for everything.
I'll make you proud.
I hear you singing in Heaven.
I love you.
Eileen

Dear Eileen,
I'm proud of you already.
Love,
Dad

Dear World,
Please listen,
I just want the suffering to stop.
Is that such a tall order?
I love you.
Eileen

The End

About the Author

Eileen Forrestal, CEO of Get Up and Go Publications Ltd, is a retired anaesthesiologist who has now embarked on a new phase of her life as an author, speaker, coach and mentor.

Having spent years in the background, both in her medical career as an anaesthesiologist, and in growing her entrepreneurial publishing business, Eileen is now coming out into the spotlight with *The Courage to Shine*.

Having struggled with her own self-expression (because of a stutter) and its impact on her self-esteem, confidence and wellbeing, it wasn't until Eileen found the courage to speak up and say what she wanted to say, that her experience of life change utterly.

Her favourite quote is "The cave you fear to enter holds the treasure you seek" (Joseph Campbell) Yes, it takes courage to shine!

Having 'hidden' in her profession for 20 years, as an anaesthesiologist, quietly putting people to sleep (with drugs), she is now in the business of 'waking people up'!

Eileen has already transformed thousands of lives, both in her medical career and through her inspirational publications. Eileen remains committed to sharing her wisdom, insight and experience to inspire and encourage others to confidently shine in their own light, awake to the potential and joy of their own unique, authentic self-expression. She shares a message of the power of words as access to healing personal suffering and promoting wellbeing.

A native of Dublin, Eileen now resides in the beautiful countryside of Sligo. She is a contributing author in *Courageous Vulnerability, Everyday Heroes, Get up and Go Heroes*, and *You are a Genius*. Her paper "Wake Up" was published in the *Journal of the Conference for Global Transformation 2020*. She has also appeared on RTE's *Dragon's Den and The Elaine Show*.

A portion of the proceeds of this book will contribute to Free To Shine – an organisation that works on preventing child trafficking in Cambodia, a country dear to Eileen's heart - through B1G1 – Business For Good.

Read more about Eileen at *https://eileenforrestal.com* and subscribe to her mailing list.

Email: *Eileen@eileenforrestal.com*
        shineyourlight@gmail.com

Follow her on Twitter: *@shineUpYourLife*
Linked-In: *Dr Eileen Forrestal*
Facebook: *Eileen Forrestal – Shine Your Light*
www.getupandgodiary.com